Making Fabric Jewelry

Making Fabric Jewelry

20+ Projects to Stitch, Fold, & Wear

Marthe Le Van

LARK CRAFTS
Asheville

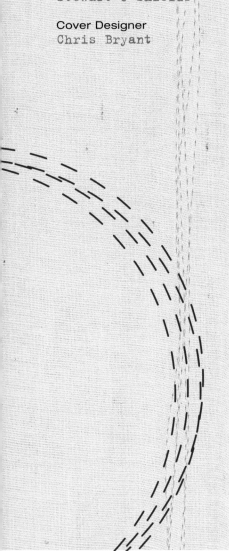

Editor
Larry Shea

Art Director
Stacey Budge-Kamison

Assistant Editor
Mark Bloom

Illustrator
Orrin Lundgren

Photographer
Stewart O'Shields

Cover Designer
Chris Bryant

LARK CRAFTS

An Imprint of Sterling Publishing
387 Park Avenue South
New York, NY 10016

If you have questions or comments about this book, please visit: larkcrafts.com

The Library of Congress has cataloged the hardcover edition as follows:

Le Van, Marthe.
    Stitched Jewels / Marthe Le Van.
        p. cm.
    Includes bibliographical references and index.
    ISBN 978-1-60059-248-5 (hc-plc with jacket : alk. paper)
    1. Jewelry Making. 2. Textile Crafts I. Title.
TT22.L52 2009
739.27--dc22
            2008036240

10 9 8 7 6 5 4 3 2 1

Published by Lark Crafts
An Imprint of Sterling Publishing Co., Inc.
387 Park Avenue South, New York, NY 10016

First Paperback Edition 2012
Text and illustrations © 2009, Lark Crafts, an Imprint of Sterling Publishing Co., Inc.
Photography © 2009, Lark Crafts, an Imprint of Sterling Publishing Co., Inc.

Previously published as *Stitched Jewels*

Distributed in Canada by Sterling Publishing,
c/o Canadian Manda Group, 165 Dufferin Street
Toronto, Ontario, Canada M6K 3H6

Distributed in the United Kingdom by GMC Distribution Services,
Castle Place, 166 High Street, Lewes, East Sussex, England BN7 1XU

Distributed in Australia by Capricorn Link (Australia) Pty Ltd.,
P.O. Box 704, Windsor, NSW 2756 Australia

Manufactured in Canada

ISBN 13: 978-1-60059-248-5 (hardcover) 978-1-4547-0415-7 (paperback)

For information about custom editions, special sales, premium and corporate purchases, please contact Sterling Special Sales Department at 800-805-5489 or specialsales@sterlingpub.com.

For information about desk and examination copies available to college and university professors, requests must be submitted to academic@larkbooks.com. Our complete policy can be found at www.larkcrafts.com.

Contents

Introduction

There's a revolution underway. There are no bullhorns or anthems or placards that demand attention, but if you look closely at the ears and arms and fingers of the women on the street, you'll see a remarkable change. Personal adornment is undergoing a makeover for the 21st century.

As the price of precious metals and gemstones skyrockets and the environmental and social costs of extracting these commodities come into question, designers are mining their imagination instead of our planet to create spectacular, innovative accessories. From street fashion to haute couture, jewelry made from alternative materials is popping up everywhere, and one of the most exciting, versatile, and responsible of all the unconventional materials is fabric. Fabric touches us everyday. We wake up between soft sheets, towel off with terry, and dress ourselves in cotton, so why not accessorize with fabric too?

Making Fabric Jewelry is a collection of 23 artful projects by top jewelry designers, all using fabric. Because the medium combines two popular pursuits—textile arts and jewelry making—and because the concept itself is nontraditional, the featured artists have diverse backgrounds and training. For example, Ellen Gerritse is a talented silversmith who shares an ornate leaf neckpiece crafted from bright mesh swatches (page 130). Deborah Boschert is known primarily as a fabric artist, and her project demonstrates a technique where layered circles of cotton are fused over a leather cord (page 42). Bethany Fields' black-and-white gingham bracelet (page 108) seems perfectly suited for someone with her theatrical training. Whatever your background, you'll love how a unique style emerges as you complete these projects.

Whether you're a connoisseur of the finest velvet or someone who simply knows that corduroy is the bumpy stuff, the Basics section in this book will help you understand the skills, supplies, and tools needed to create these fabulous accessories. You'll learn some basic metalworking techniques like wire wrapping and attaching crimp beads, and you'll have the opportunity to practice classic hand-sewn stitching. Then you can run with it—precisely following every instruction or veering off the path to make it your own. No prior knowledge of jewelry making or sewing is necessary, but advanced jewelers will enjoy the diversity of materials and processes.

One of the perks of crafting with fabric is the sheer quantity of materials to choose from, each one conjuring up a different association: cotton, tulle, silk, felt, lace, denim, satin, and the list goes on. The collection of projects in *Making Fabric Jewelry* represents amazing variety in this regard. Steven James, for instance, molds stiff cotton thread into a sculpted necklace (page 54) while Miyuki Cook transforms vintage kimono silk from the Kaga region of Japan into exquisite hoop earrings (page 58). Of course, you can personalize the designs with your own eco-friendly, recycled fabric or local thrift store finds. Stash divers and scrap hoarders, this is your calling.

The scope of project styles is broad enough to suit any occasion—Karen Lauseng's felt cuff bracelet (page 62) is great for a casual stroll in the park, while Jennifer Kahn's fashion-forward, silver-stitched earrings (page 124) complement your next invitation-only gallery opening—but none are out of reach. The skill levels range from a super easy, no-sew approach, where all you need is a pair of scissors or an iron, to intermediate machine stitching, quilting, and stuffing. If you're looking for inspiration, the book's extensive gallery of fabric jewel images will spark your creative flair.

Fabric jewelry is a natural combination of material and form. It's comfortable. It's economical. It's deeply creative and as stylish as all get out. So what are you waiting for? Tune in (your imagination), turn on (to fabric), and join the revolution!

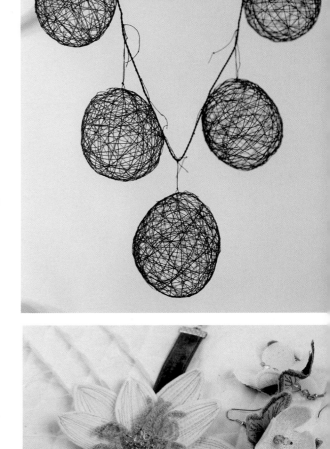

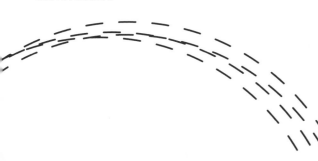

Basics

The words "fabric jewelry" might sound strange to your ear, but the pieces you'll see in this book will astound your eyes. Using fabric—an unexpected but versatile material—to create stylish and clever necklaces, bracelets, and brooches will delight all your senses. The textures, the color combinations, the fanciful designs all contribute to fantastic and fantastically inspirational jewelry, ranging from whimsical everyday accessories to glamorous pieces for special occasions. If you don't believe me, just flip through the book and see for yourself.

You don't have to be an experienced sewer to make these fresh and fashionable projects; the techniques are quite simple. This chapter will teach you everything you need to know to create not only the jewelry in this book, but also to experiment on your own. In fact, I hope you use these projects as a jumping off point for your own unique designs.

But before you venture into uncharted waters, take some time to learn what it takes to put these pieces together. It'll be time well spent.

Material Matters

When making fabric jewelry, the first pleasure is choosing the fabric. This section covers the types of material you'll use for the projects in this book, from simple cotton and corduroy to tulle and kimono silk.

The fabrics run a wide and colorful gamut. Because you are not making garments, you don't have to be as concerned with pesky details such as whether the material is machine washable or dry-clean only. And, since the projects are relatively small, you can easily use scraps from your sewing stash, repurpose old clothing or vintage linen, or even find perfect swatches from a remnant table. As you stroll through the fabric store, don't overlook the drapery and upholstery sections. You might find some beautiful jewelry materials waiting for you there. Let your design sense and personal preferences guide you.

The fabrics can be woven or knit. You can use natural fibers—such as cotton, linen, wool, and silk—as well as synthetic fibers like polyester, acrylic, and nylon. Rayon straddles these two categories because it's synthesized from wood pulp; it's manmade, but from a natural source. Other synthetic fabrics are made from sources such as petroleum products, and many fabrics are blends of both natural and synthetic fibers. Here's a closer look at some frequently used fabrics.

Cotton—The cotton plant grows in subtropic regions around the world, including the Americas, India, and Africa. Spun into yarn or thread and used to make textiles, cotton is the most widely used natural-fiber fabric. Cotton is durable, easy to sew, and has a soft, natural feel. It comes in an endless array of colors and prints. The sheerest and crispest cotton cloth is called *organdy*.

Linen—Linen is lustrous, strong, and durable. Like cotton, you can find it in an assortment of wonderful colors and prints.

Felt—As materials go, felt is pretty much foolproof. It's non-woven, soft, doesn't ravel, and has no right side or wrong side to worry about. Traditionally, felt is made from wool, though the felt you see in craft stores is usually synthetic.

Fleece—Call it what you will—microfleece, micrafleece, or just plain old fleece—this synthetic textile is a soft, napped insulating fabric developed to mimic the warmth of wool, but without its weight. Fleece is available in different thicknesses and is often made entirely from recycled materials.

Wear It Again, Sam!

Vintage and recycled fabrics are eco-friendly (and eco-nomical!) materials for jewelry making. Because you won't ever require a large amount of yardage, you can find supplies almost everywhere. Have a stash of old fabric scraps? Moth-chomped sweaters, beloved old blazers, pillowcases, T-shirts, or even tea towels will work! They are ripe to be refashioned. If the pickings are slim around your abode, check out local thrift stores, second-hand shops, and garage sales for fabulous fabric finds.

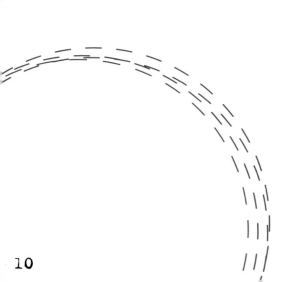

Wool—Speaking of wool, this classic fabric can be fuzzy or smooth, fleecy or ribbed. It's soft, durable, and very absorbent.

Canvas—This heavy-duty fabric is used for sails, tents, and backpacks. It's a great choice for making sturdier jewelry projects. In the United States, canvas is graded by weight (ounces per square yard) and by number. The numbers run in reverse of the weight, so number 10 canvas is lighter than number 4.

Corduroy—Woven and twisted fibers lie parallel to each other to form corduroy's distinct pattern. Sometimes, a channel of base fabric is visible between the tufted cords. The width of the cord is referred to as the *wale*. Like canvas, grading by number is used for corduroy, with a lower number indicating a thicker wale width.

Silk—Sturdy fabric is well and good, but to add a little luxury to your projects, try silk. It offers a refined touch and has a lustrous look. Choose a medium-weight silk; it can stand up to some wear and tear. Silk ravels easily, so the seams need to be finished, unless you want a frayed look. Be sure to sew with a sharp, new needle. Several projects in this book use vintage silk kimono cloth to great effect.

Satin—Satin has a glossy face, a dull back, and a soft, slippery texture. It can be made from acetate, rayon, nylon, or silk fibers.

Organza—A sheer fabric traditionally made from silk, organza is now more commonly woven with synthetic filament fibers such as polyester or nylon. It has a thin, plain weave and is popular for bridal wear, eveningwear, and sheer curtains.

Tulle—This is a delicate, lightweight netting made of various fibers, including silk, nylon, and rayon. Tulle is available in a rainbow of colors and is often used for veils, wedding gowns, and ballet tutus.

Lace—Lace is an open, ornamental fabric with a pattern of surface holes. The fabric can be hand- or machine-made; it can be fine or heavy. Find a lace pattern that suits you, and you'll discover how versatile lace really is.

Ribbon—You're not making bed quilts, you're making fabric jewelry, so ribbon is great as a base material as well as an accent. Experiment with different varieties and widths of ribbon, such as hand-dyed silk, lush velvet, grosgrain, and even retro rickrack.

Thea Starr
Magenta Blooms, 2007
7.6 x 15.2 x 1.3 cm
Kanzami, silk, hair prong, soutache;
folded, hand dyed, mounted
Photo by artist

Selecting Colors and Patterns

When choosing fabric, you usually consider qualities like workability and durability (yawn!). Even when you are deciding about texture and contrast, you're still making mundane choices. When it comes to picking colors, however, the most essential quality is fun. Keep in mind, though, that the most important aspect of picking colors is how well they work together in your design.

Values, also known as tones, refer to the lightness or darkness of a color, not its particular hue. When you combine colors, you can choose between medium or darker tones or lighter, more pastel values. Whether you seek to match all the values in a piece or create dramatic juxtapositions is up to you.

Besides the colors themselves, you can choose from solids, stripes, and patterns. While I encourage you to experiment, just be sure of the effect the mix produces. Fortunately, you can hold bits of fabric next to each other to compare the combination. Make sure everything works together before you start cutting and sewing.

From Alpaca to Zibeline

There is a ridiculous amount of different fabrics out there, all of them begging to be used in your next jewelry creation. Of the 100 fabric types listed below (and there are more … many, many more), you'll find some that are quite familiar and others that are completely unknown to you. Boldly explore different fibers and weaves in your fabric search. Don't be shy; a wonderful world awaits you!

- Alpaca
- Angora
- Baft
- Batiste
- Bouclé
- Broadcloth
- Brocade
- Buckram
- Bunting
- Burlap
- Calico
- Cambric
- Cashmere
- Challis
- Chambray
- Chamois
- Charmeuse
- Chenille
- Chiffon
- Chino
- Chintz
- Cordovan
- Corduroy
- Crepe
- Crinoline

- Damask
- Denim
- Dimity
- Duck
- Duffel
- Dungaree
- Dupion
- Eyelet
- Faille
- Flannel
- Foulard
- Gabardine
- Georgette
- Gingham
- Grosgrain
- Herringbone
- Hopsack
- Houndstooth
- Jacquard
- Jean
- Jersey
- Kente
- Lamé
- Lawn
- Macintosh

- Mackinaw
- Madras
- Matelassé
- Melton
- Merino
- Mohair
- Moiré
- Moleskin
- Mousseline
- Muslin
- Needlecord
- Organdy
- Organza
- Osnaburg
- Ottoman
- Oxford
- Paisley
- Panné
- Pashmina
- Percale
- Piqué
- Plissé
- Pongee
- Poplin
- Ramie

- Sateen
- Satin
- Scrim
- Seersucker
- Shantung
- Sharkskin
- Stockinette
- Taffeta
- Tarlatan
- Terry cloth
- Ticking
- Toile
- Tricot
- Tulle
- Tussah
- Tweed
- Twill
- Velour
- Velvet
- Velveteen
- Vicuna
- Voile
- Woolsey
- Worsted
- Zibeline

13

Sewing Gear

In this section, you'll find information on the sewing tools and materials you need to make the projects in this book. This includes the types of scissors you'll need as well as the importance of straight pins, needles, rotary cutters, seam rippers, and sewing machines. You'll also find valuable information on both the necessary and optional supplies, like thread, interfacing, snaps, fabric glue, markers, and batting.

For some of you, this will be a quick refresher, but for others, it's everything you need to know to be "in the sew," and you'll want to refer to these pages often. Either way, you should start by assembling your Basic Tool Kit (see sidebar). Most projects call for these items so, novice or not, you'll want to have them at hand. Chances are, you already have many of the supplies listed, so dig through your drawers and closets before hitting the stores.

Basic Tool Kit

- Sharp sewing scissors (for fabric)
- Sharp fine-tipped scissors (for detailed work)
- Craft scissors (for paper)
- Measuring tape
- Ruler
- Straight pins
- Hand-sewing needles

- Thread (in a variety of colors)
- Insulating material
- Scrap paper (for patterns)
- Pencil with an eraser
- Iron
- Sewing machine
- Water-soluble fabric marker

Measure and Mark

For measuring large pieces of fabric, a measuring tape is all you need. A transparent quilting ruler, though, handles several jobs without breaking a sweat. Use one to measure and mark precise distances, determine a line perpendicular to a fabric edge, and guide a rotary cutter straight and sure.

Use a water-soluble fabric-marking pen or pencil to mark lines for cutting, embroidering, and sewing. The ink should vanish with plain water, but to be certain, test your pen on a scrap piece of the fabric you will be using first. Sometimes the dyes in some fabrics can make the ink hard to remove. In addition to fabric-marking pens, a variety of traditional and newfangled fabric chalks are also available.

Cut It Out

Good quality, sharp sewing scissors are an essential part of your kit. You'll need two pairs. For basic cutting, a pair of 7- or 8-inch (18 to 20 cm) dressmaker's bent-handled shears will do the job. The design of the handle allows the fabric to lay flat as you cut. To cut tight curves and do other detail work like trimming seams, a pair of fine-tipped, 4- or 5-inch (10 to 13 cm) sewing scissors is the way to go.

Never let anyone—including yourself in a hurried moment—use your good sewing scissors to cut paper. The wood fibers in the paper will dull the blades quickly and make them useless with fabric.

Just as sewing scissors are meant for fabric and thread, craft scissors are perfect for paper. You'll need a pair to cut out the templates in several patchwork projects. Find ones that feel comfortable in your hand. A short to moderate length is best for making fine cuts on curves and corners.

Pinking shears have a serrated edge that leaves a zigzag pattern, which can help limit fabric fraying. You can also use them to make decorative cuts and edges. Pinking shears aren't essential, but you'll wish you had them if you don't.

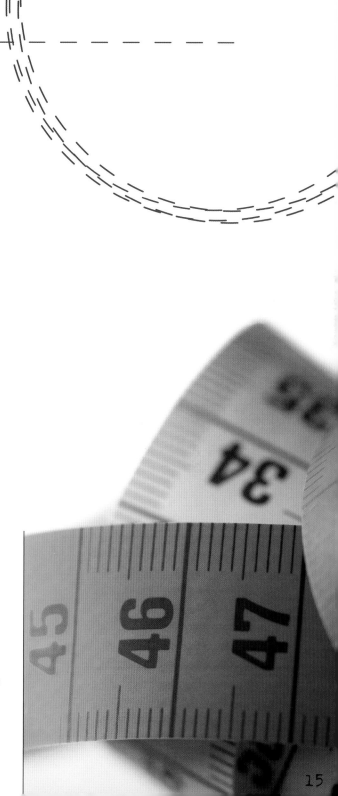

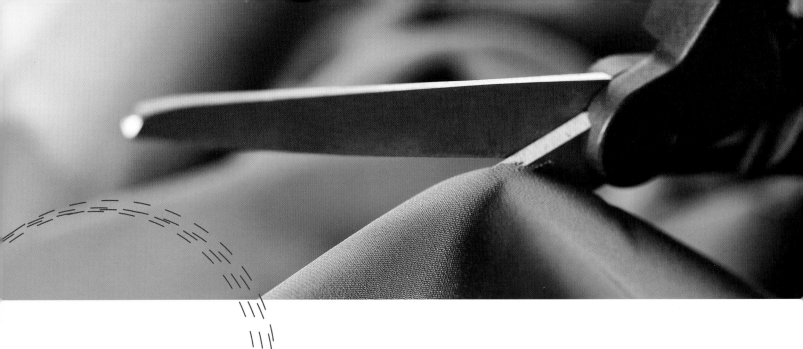

Together with a transparent ruler or straightedge and a self-healing cutting mat, a rotary cutter makes short work of cutting straight fabric pieces—lots of them—to just the right size. If you've never used a rotary cutter, try one at your local fabric store. In general, the larger the blade, the easier it is to cut fabric. A mid-size cutter will do the job for the projects in this book.

TIP: Why do rotary cutters work so beautifully? They're sharp! Here are two safety tips to remember. First, keep the safety latch in place when the cutter is not in use. Second, always cut away from your fingers.

Hold Everything!

Basic dressmaker's pins hold fabric pieces together. The longer pins with plastic or glass heads are easier to handle and easier on your fingertips. They're also easier to spot and remove as you stitch your way near them. It's a good idea to have a few safety pins in a couple of different sizes on hand. You won't need many, since the projects in this book tend to be smaller than full-scale garments.

Needle Knowledge

A variety pack of hand and sewing machine needles should include all of the types you'll need to sew the projects in this book. Use a finer needle for lightweight fabrics and a thicker, longer needle for thicker fabrics. Regular woven fabrics and silks do best with the sharp pointed needles known—unsurprisingly—as "sharps." Round-tipped needles, or "ball-points," are better for knit materials. The rounded point pushes between the fibers without piercing them, minimizing the possibility of a run or pull in the fabric.

Some projects ask specifically for an embroidery needle. It has a longer eye to make it easier to thread several strands of embroidery floss at once. You can use embroidery needles for detailing and for regular hand stitching as well.

Tired of licking and twisting thread ends trying to get them—steady now!—through a needle's eye? Instead, just use that handy helper known as a needle threader. Insert its wire loop through the eye of the needle, insert the thread in the loop, pull back, and you're ready to sew.

Everybody makes mistakes once in a while, so a seam ripper is another handy tool. It removes incorrect stitches easily, without anyone being the wiser.

Heather Rathbun
Accordion Jewelry, 2007

Each clasp, 3 x 1.5 x 1.5 cm

Polyester organza, interfacing, sterling silver, magnets; heat set, layered

Photo by artist

CRAFT NEEDLES

Get a Grip

Bargain thread is no bargain. To create strong seams, use good quality, multipurpose polyester thread for hand and machine sewing. It is strong, durable, and versatile. A good-quality all-cotton thread is suitable for sewing with woven, natural fabrics like cotton. Thread is manufactured in a huge number of colors, including clear, metallic, and variegated varieties.

Embroidery floss is a decorative thread that comes in six loosely twisted strands. You can buy it in cotton, silk, rayon, and other fibers, and in every color of the rainbow. Use an embroidery needle with floss to sew decorative stitches.

TIP: Choose thread in a color that complements your fabric. A thread that's slightly darker than the fabric is less likely to stand out. For decorative elements such as embroidery work, you might want a highly contrasting thread color to announce, "Hey, look at all the sewing I did!"

Fray retardant can be found in both liquid and spray-on applications. This product binds with fibers to prevent unraveling. It's convenient to use on seams in tight spaces where you can't zigzag to overcast and for sealing the edges of appliqués.

Besides sewing with thread, the projects in this book call for a variety of methods to connect pieces of fabric together, including spray adhesive, white glue, glue sticks, and hot glue with a glue gun. The right product depends on the strength, durability, and setting quickness the project requires.

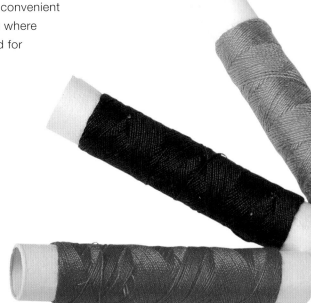

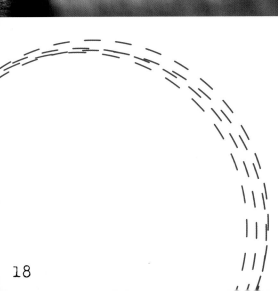

Sewing Machine Savvy

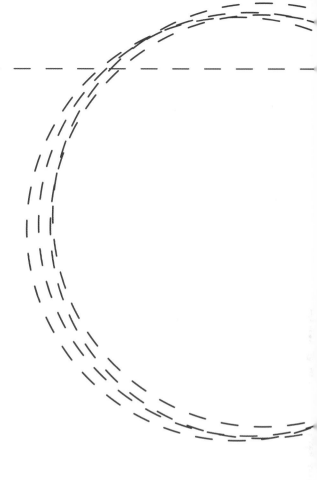

You can't beat a sewing machine for speed and efficiency. This fantastic invention creates a lockstitch when the thread from the needle (on top of the machine) and the thread from the bobbin (inside the machine) loop together in the fabric. When you sew, this action happens at a remarkable speed.

A typical sewing machine has a spool (or spools) and thread guides to hold and guide the thread, a hand wheel, a needle, needle plate and feed dogs, tension disks, presser foot and presser foot lever, bobbin and bobbin winder. It also has controls to adjust the stitch width, stitch length, thread tension, and presser foot pressure. All of these parts work in synch to create the lockstitch. Although they share common characteristics, sewing machines vary from manufacturer to manufacturer. Your sewing machine manual is the best source of information for your particular model. It will have detailed information about threading the machine, winding the bobbin, adjusting the stitch width and length, and selecting any specialty stitches.

Always keep extra sewing machine needles on hand. Just as sharp scissors make cutting fabric a piece of cake, it's easier to sew with sharp needles. It's a good idea to use a new needle at the beginning of each sewing project. Needles are cheap, especially compared to your time and energy.

Supporting Roles

You can add support and structure to your projects with interfacing. While there are several types, you'll usually use *fusible* interfacing, which you apply to fabric with the heat and pressure of an iron. Paper-backed fusible web is a heat-set material that bonds on both sides, making it ideal for attaching appliqués.

Beyond its everyday job of removing wrinkles, an iron can handle a number of other tasks. Use it to press seams open and to apply interfacing, appliqués, and photo-transfer sheets to fabric. Never use steam when ironing paper.

When a jewelry project requires you to fill the space between two layers of fabric, a common choice is cotton batting. It's durable, easy to work with, and available in different thicknesses. Felt is another option, depending on the desired thickness and feel of the project. Some projects require stuffing. Polyester fiberfill is a good choice and it keeps its shape well. Grade one fiberfill is soft, resilient, and non-allergenic; it's readily available at craft and sewing stores.

Closing Comments

Beautiful, beautiful buttons! For some, collecting them is a joyful addiction, but others relish them for their craft applications. Use them as closures for your jewelry or let them stand alone as design elements. Flat buttons are less likely to get snagged or caught on clothing.

Snaps are the most practical closure when making small items. You can use traditional black or silver sew-on snaps, or more decorative snaps when you want extra embellishment.

Get Stitching

Now that you're familiar with the types of fabrics, threads, notions, and tools these projects require, it's time to discuss the fine art and craft of sewing: forming stitches, seaming, ironing, tying knots, and working with fusible interfacing. If you're new to the craft, this section will get you started, but only practice will make you proficient. (That's why you bought this book, right?) If you're an old hand with a needle and thread, a quick scan of the following pages will let you know if you've forgotten anything important.

Hand Sewing 101

Even the most dedicated sewing machine enthusiast will occasionally need to sew some stitches by hand. This section presents the hand stitches you'll need to know for the projects in this book. Some of the stitches can even be used as surface embellishment.

First Thing First: Threading a Sewing Needle

You can accomplish this seemingly impossible task with a few simple steps. If this trick still eludes you, use a needle threader (page 17).

1. Hold the needle upright with one hand, and rotate it in your fingers until you can see the eye.

2. Hold the cut thread about ¾ inch (2 cm) from the end with the fingers of your other hand. Push the thread through the eye of the needle until about ½ inch (1.5 cm) extends beyond the eye.

3. Pull about a third of the thread length through the eye for a single thread; pull half through to match the cut ends if you need a double thread.

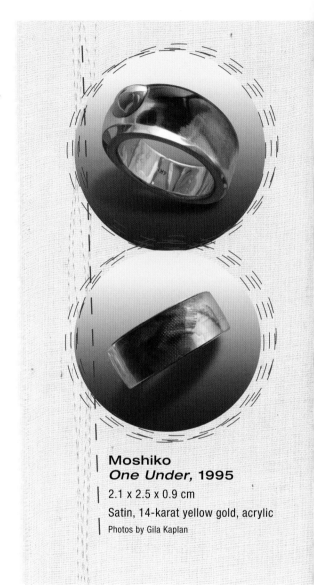

Moshiko
One Under, 1995
2.1 x 2.5 x 0.9 cm
Satin, 14-karat yellow gold, acrylic
Photos by Gila Kaplan

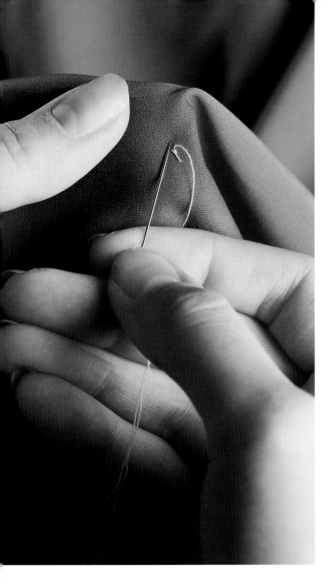

TIP: If you have trouble threading the needle, the following tricks may help:

- Place the needle in front of a white surface to make the eye more visible.
- Stiffen the thread end by moistening it or running it through beeswax.
- Dip the end of the thread into a bottle of red nail polish and allow it to dry. Colored polish makes the thread easier to see and provides a slicker end for threading.
- Spray your fingertips with hair spray and stiffen the tip of the thread by rolling it back and forth in your fingers.
- Try a needle with a larger eye or use a needle threader.

Classic Stitches

Before you start any hand stitch, tie a knot at the end of the thread. This will hold your stitches in place. Also, when you finish a seam, take a few stitches in the same place to secure the thread, and then snip off the excess thread. These two techniques will keep your stitches from loosening.

Backstitch—This basic hand stitch is used to create a strong seam (figure 1) because it is least likely to unravel. It's also good for outlining shapes or text. Sew over the same stitches, backward and forward, to lock the thread, especially at the end of a seam.

Basting—This loose stitch is a way to temporarily secure two pieces of fabric. It is the same as a running stitch (figure 4), except that you make it with very long stitches that you can remove easily once the permanent stitch is in place.

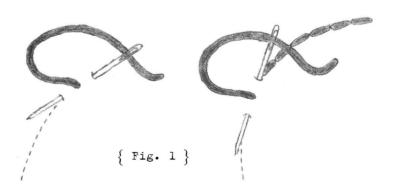

{ Fig. 1 }

Blanket stitch—This is a decorative and functional stitch that you can use to accentuate an edge or attach a cut shape to a layer of fabric (figure 2).

Buttonhole—Similar to the blanket stitch, the buttonhole stitch forms a knot at the fabric edge so it holds up extremely well to wear and tear (figure 3).

Running stitch—The running stitch is as basic as it sounds—a single thread drawn in a straight line through the fabric at evenly spaced intervals (figure 4). It is frequently used for gathering fabrics together.

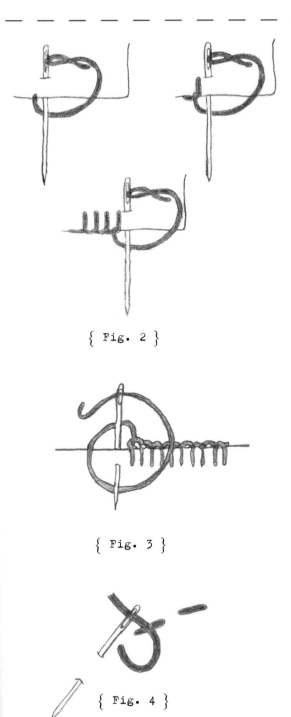

{ Fig. 2 }

{ Fig. 3 }

{ Fig. 4 }

Evelien Sipkes
Necklace, Queens Coral, 2005

3 x 4 x 21 cm

Silk, copper, porcelain, beads, velvet; sewn

Photo by Dolph van Stapele

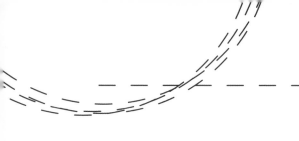

Slipstitch—This is another basic stitch, often used to sew openings closed. Slip the needle through one end of the open seam to anchor the thread, then take a small stitch through the fold and pull the needle through. Insert the needle directly opposite the stitch you just made in the other piece of fabric, and pull the thread through that fold. Keep going until you're finished (figure 5).

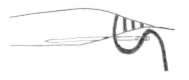

{ Fig. 5 }

Straight stitch—Used to sew fabrics together, the straight stitch is the most important of all the stitches; it is the foundation stitch for both hand- and machine-sewing. Draw a thread in a straight line from the right side of the fabric to the back and then back to the right side again, repeat to finish the seam.

Topstitch—This stitch is similar to a straight stitch, except instead of joining two pieces of fabric, you use it primarily as a decorative stitch to add detail and embellishment.

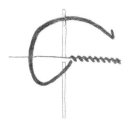

Whipstitch—The whipstitch, also called an overcast stitch, is used to bind edges to prevent raveling. Sew the stitches over the edge of the fabric (figure 6).

{ Fig. 6 }

Machine Stitching

Let's discuss the basics. When you use a sewing machine, make sure the stitch tension is properly set for the type of fabric you are using (some sewing machines automatically adjust the tension). Sew a practice or test seam on a scrap of fabric before sewing the real jewelry fabric. Then follow these steps:

1. Pin the fabric pieces with right sides together, the edges aligned, and the straight pins at right angles to the seam.

2. Align the cut edges with the desired seam allowance marking on the machine throat plate. Stitch forward and then in reverse two to three stitches to lock the thread. Continue machine-stitching to form the seam, removing the pins as you go. At the end of the seam, stitch two to three stitches in reverse again to prevent the thread from unraveling.

3. To stitch around a corner, stitch slowly as you approach the corner. Keep the needle down at the corner point, lift the presser foot and pivot the fabric. Lower the presser foot and continue the seam.

4. When you are stitching by machine, be sure to let the machine pull the fabric along, you simply guide it.

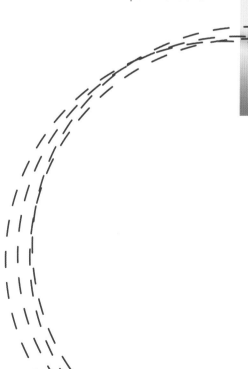

Embellishment Techniques

The following special touches bring a wealth of charm to your jewelry. Most of them can be added before or after assembly. When you're thinking about embellishment, don't forget your sewing machine's selection of decorative stitches. With just the twist of a knob, you can add new dimension to your design. The Sun-Kissed Lemons project (page 112) shows decorative stitch embellishment.

Fusing Appliqués

Appliqué is the fancy name for a decorative fabric cutout applied to the right side of another fabric. Appliqués add texture and extra visual interest to your design. One of the fastest ways to make and apply an appliqué is to use lightweight paper-backed fusible web. Here's how to apply an appliqué to your design:

1. Apply a piece of paper-backed fusible web to a piece of fabric that is slightly larger than the appliqué design. Follow the manufacturer's instructions for applying the fusible web to the fabric. Do not remove the paper backing. Draw or trace the outline of the appliqué directly on the paper, and then cut out the paper, fusible web, and fabric together.

2. Remove the paper backing and position the appliqué on your fabric. Press the appliqué with an iron, again following the manufacturer's instructions.

3. If necessary, stitch around the appliqué to prevent the fabric edge from raveling with a hand-stitched appliqué stitch or a machine appliqué stitch. Another way to prevent raveling is to apply fray retardant to the edges of the appliqué before affixing it to the fabric.

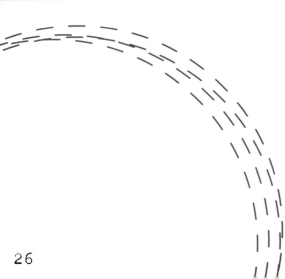

Free-Motion Stitching

This technique is like coloring with thread. Consult your sewing machine manual for the required machine settings and presser feet. To prepare most machines for free-motion stitching, you'll need to drop the sewing machine's feed dogs and change to the correct presser foot. This allows you to move the fabric in all directions with your hands and stitch freely over the fabric.

Start with a sharp new needle. Try to relax and sew smoothly at a medium pace. There are no lines or patterns to follow, no right or wrong. Enjoy the process and let your creativity guide you.

Quilting

Quilting creates a decorative, textured effect and the process is simple. Sandwich batting between two layers of fabric, and hand- or machine-stitch through all the layers. How much easier could it be? The creativity comes through the choice of fabric, colors, and patterns that you stitch together. Many quilters repeat designs or create a larger design out of smaller pieces.

Applying Snaps

You can't beat sew-on snaps for pure practicality—a few stitches and they're secure. Decorative snaps are a design booster; some are attached with a hammer, while others need a special tool. Follow the manufacturer's instructions and you can't go wrong. If you place a small square of interfacing behind the fabric at the snap location, you will increase the durability of the fabric under the snap.

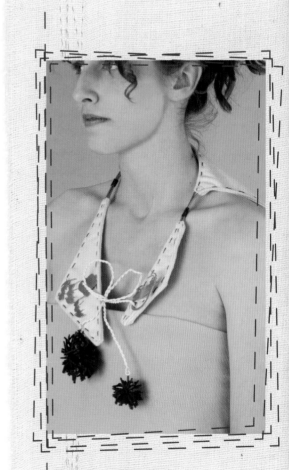

Vanessa Neily
***Remember Not To Lie*, 2008**
28 x 22 x 18 cm
Titanium, brass, copper, cotton; powder coated, flocked, screen printed
Photo by Heather Rathbun

Lily Yung
Blue Boa, 2006

10 x 10 x 80 cm

Wool felt; die cut, hand assembled

Photo by Yunla-Swavek Sienkiewicz

Finding Your Findings

All of the little components—usually metal—that help keep a piece of jewelry together, wearable, and secure are called *findings*. The most recognizable findings include clasps, earring wires and nuts, jump rings, and bails.

Ready-made findings are manufactured in a range of styles and are available wherever craft, jewelry, and beading supplies are sold. You can also make many jewelry findings by hand. Well-designed and well-crafted custom findings always enhance the appearance of handmade jewelry.

It's the Little Things

There's a saying that you shouldn't sweat the little things, but in fabric jewelry, it's often the little things that make a big difference. Findings fall into that category. Listed here are many of the findings worth "sweating over"—in a good way, of course.

Clasps—Clasps connect and secure the ends of a necklace or bracelet. They are available in an ever-growing number of styles, including box, fish hook, toggle, lobster claw, S-hook, hook-and-eye, and magnetic.

Cones or caps—Generally, you use these findings at the end of a jewelry strand to hide knots. They are made out of metal and come in a huge variety of designs. Find the ones that fit your style.

Crimp tubes and beads—Crimp tubes and crimp beads connect wires to findings. See page 35 to learn how they work. You can also use crimp covers, which open and then close over crimp beads to hide them.

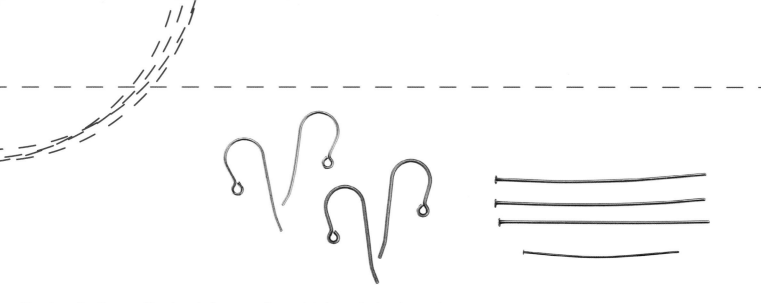

Earring findings—Simply put, these are the metal pieces that make earrings wearable. Earring findings include French wires, kidney wires, lever-back wires, clips, screws, nuts, and posts. Like most findings, these jewelry components can be purchased or handmade.

Eye pins—You use eye pins to make beaded links. An eye pin is a straight piece of wire with a simple loop at one end, sort of like a monocle for a tiny doll.

Head pins—Use head pins to string beads and create dangles. A simple head pin is a straight wire with a tiny disk at one end that holds a bead in place. Ball-end head pins have a sphere, rather than a disk at the end.

Jump rings—Wire circles, called jump rings, are a simple way to hold jewelry components together. The rings are split so you can open and close them using two pairs of flat-nose pliers. Although jump rings are commercially manufactured, you can easily make your own from almost any gauge of wire.

Pin backs—Metal pin backs come in several shapes in order to accommodate the shape of the jewelry form they need to support. Standard brooch findings resemble safety pins. Stick pin findings have a long, straight wire with a pointed end and a clutch. Scatter pin findings have a short pointed wire and a larger, round clutch. There are many ways to attach a pin back, including good jewelry glue, hand stitching, and soldering.

Split rings—These rings are more like tiny key rings than jump rings. Their split ends overlap rather than meet. You can use split rings interchangeably with jump rings.

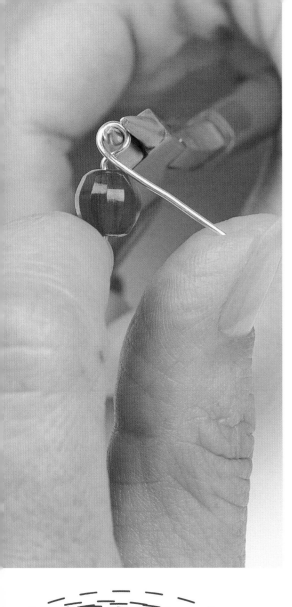

Tools for Jewels

Pliers, wire cutters, and hammers? What exactly do you need to make the gorgeous stitched jewels in this book?

While some jewelry projects in this book include no metal work at all, others rely on simple skills that you can learn quickly. The good news is that you don't need to run out and buy new metalworking tools. You also don't need to master a lot of new techniques. All you really need to do is read through the following pages that list the recommended materials and methods.

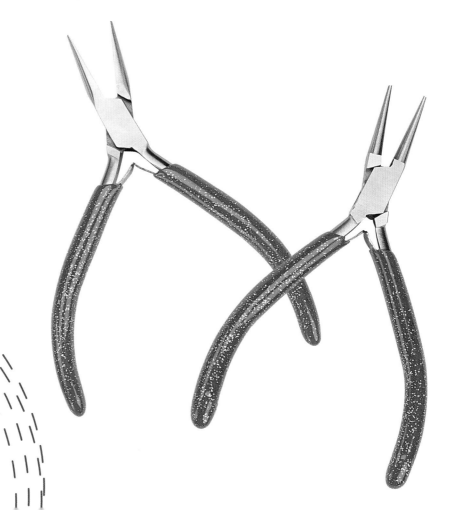

Metal Fundamentals

To make your fabric jewelry really pop, add sparkling accents to the design. Silver and gold are undoubtedly the most eye-catching, most loved, and most traditional metals used in jewelry. Unfortunately, they're also some of the most expensive materials. Other options include copper, aluminum, brass, bronze, and stainless steel, whose luscious colors combined with their lower price make them equally appealing.

Most of the metal—which is readily available from jewelry, bead, and metal suppliers—is sold in two common forms: flat sheets and wire rolls.

Flat sheets of both precious and base metals are manufactured and sold in different sizes. The thickness of the metal is referred to as its gauge, and inversely, the thinner the metal, the higher its gauge number.

Metal wire is manufactured with many different profiles and in many different thicknesses. Round wire is the most common shape, but there is also half round, square, triangular, and more. Like sheet metal, the thickness of wire is measured using the gauge system. Metal tubing is a hollow metal cylinder, manufactured and sold with different wall thicknesses and diameters.

Cut, Bend, Shape & Smooth

There are many ways to manipulate metal for your jewelry, and not all of them involve acting like a blacksmith or wearing a helmet (although safety goggles are always a good idea). This section lists some of the tools you'll need for the metalwork techniques in this book.

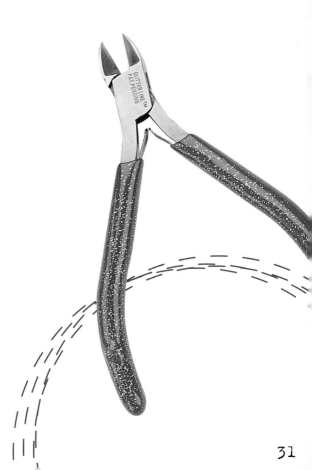

Wire cutters and metal shears—Flush-cutting a length of wire involves using the flat, or flush, side of wire cutters to make a cut so the wire end is flat. Cut a metal sheet with handheld metal shears for both straight and curved lines. Shears with smaller blades allow you to cut more intricate contours and patterns.

Åsa Halldin
Ruth, 2005

7 x 7 x 10 cm

Flax thread, cotton sheeting; woven,
photo printing

Photos by Adrian Nordenborg

Jeweler's pliers—Although pliers come in many forms, the shape of their jaw identifies most of them. Round-nose pliers have fully rounded jaws that taper up from the base. Chain-nose pliers are round on the outside of the jaw, but flat on the inside, tapering up to a point. Flat-nose pliers have flat and flush interior surfaces while the exterior surfaces of their jaws are flat and angled. Round-nose, chain-nose, and flat-nose pliers are commonly made of stainless steel or tool steel. They are available in short and long jaw lengths. Although these three types of pliers will handle most jobs, there are many other specialty pliers that are worth investigating.

Hammers—A chasing hammer is specifically designed and weighted for metal-working. Its head is made of polished steel and has two faces with different shapes. One face is wide, smooth, and slightly convex. The opposite end is ball-shaped. Mallets are exceptional tools for forming, bending, and flattening metal. Their greatest advantage is that they move metal without marring, scratching, or damaging its surface.

Mandrels—A mandrel is any type of sturdy form around which you can shape or size metal. Commercial mandrels are made of metal or wood. Ring mandrels are tapered and marked with standard ring sizes. Bracelet mandrels have a gradual taper without markings, and necklace mandrels are designed to show how a piece will drape on the neck. Feel free to use any common household item as a mandrel. Dowels and rods, even pencils, knitting needles, chopsticks, and rolling pins are practical stand-ins.

Files—Filing and sanding are necessary for smoothing rough wire, tube ends, and sheet metal edges. Files come with many different profiles, including flat, barrette, half round, and square. You can also use emery paper. The "cut" size of a file ranges from very coarse to very fine. Short needle files make a fine cut, perfect for finishing and smoothing small metal elements, and their thin shape makes it easy to reach into tight areas. As you file, touch the edge of the metal occasionally to check for rough spots.

Super Simple Metalwork

It's easy to add metal elements to fabric jewelry, even if you're new to metal
jewelry making. There are only a handful of skills you'll need to know to complete
the projects in this book. Refer to the following step-by-step techniques, and you'll
be ready in no time.

Wrapping Wire

Coiling, or tightly wrapping, wire is used primarily in this book for attaching one
wire to another, creating decorative coils and jump rings. Start by grasping the
base wire tightly in one hand. Hold the wrapping wire with your other hand and
make one wrap. Reposition your hands so you can continue to wrap the wire in
tight revolutions around the base wire.

{ Fig. 1 }

{ Fig. 2 }

Wire loops come in two versions: simple and wrapped.

Making Simple Wire Loops

1. Use chain-nose pliers to make a 90° angle bend, ⅜ inch (1 cm) from the end of the wire; or if you're using the loop to secure a bead (as for a bead dangle), cut the wire ⅜ inch (1 cm) from the top of the bead, and make the 90° angle bend right at the top of the bead (figure 1).

2. Use round-nose pliers to grasp the wire end and roll the pliers until the wire touches the 90° angle bend (figure 2).

Making Wrapped Loops

1. Use chain-nose pliers to make a 90° angle bend in the wire 2 inches (5.1 cm) from one wire end (or ¼ inch [6 mm] from the top of a bead) (figure 3).

2. Use round-nose pliers to grasp the bend and shape the wire over the pliers' top jaw.

3. Reposition the pliers so the bottom jaw is in the loop and swing the wire underneath to form a partial loop (figure 4).

4. Use chain-nose pliers or your fingers to wrap the wire in a tight coil down the stem (figure 5). Trim the excess wire close to the wrap, and use chain-nose pliers to tighten the wire end.

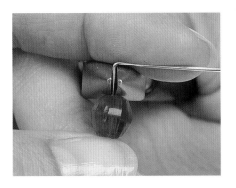

{ Fig. 3 }

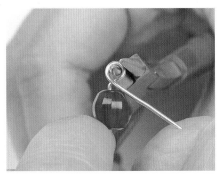

{ Fig. 4 }

{ Fig. 5 }

TIP: You can easily and securely attach a wrapped loop to another loop or chain link. First form the loop, pass the wire end through the place you want to attach it, and then make the wrap. The loops will be permanently attached.

Attaching Crimp Beads

Crimping wire and crimp beads are used to attach wire to a finding (like a clasp). Follow these steps to master this stringing technique:

1. String one crimp bead and the finding onto the wire. Pass the wire back through the crimp bead in the opposite direction.

2. Slide the crimp bead against the finding so it's snug, but not so tight that the wire can't move freely.

3. Squeeze the crimp bead with the back U-shaped notch in a pair of crimping pliers.

4. Turn the crimp bead at a 90° angle, and nestle it into the front notch of the pliers. Gently squeeze the bead so it collapses on itself into a nicely shaped tube.

Adding Jump Rings

Jump rings make quick, easy, and reliable connections between jewelry parts. Here are a few tips for working with them.

- To open and close a jump ring, move the ends from side to side on the same plane.
- Open a jump ring only as wide as necessary to insert the objects being joined; otherwise, the ring's shape might become distorted.

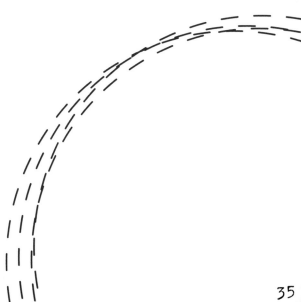

Tiny Shiny Things

It is the vast array of embellishments that makes the jewelry designs in *Making Fabric Jewelry* entirely unique and captivating. Beads, crystals, buttons, and other tiny shiny things come in a wide variety of shapes, colors, and sizes. When incorporated into the 23 great designs featured in this book, they show an amazing range of versatility. Their strength and power as design elements range from lending soft and delicate nuances to giving bold and colorful shouts.

A Beaded World

Thai silver, carved bone, semiprecious gem nuggets, vintage plastic, lamp worked glass are just a few of the incredible variety of beads available; they indicate the continued (and growing!) appeal of this oh-so-seductive material. You can buy beads, which are measured in millimeters, individually or on strands that are usually 16 inches (40.6 cm) long.

Crystal beads, clear or colored, are made from leaded glass. They are usually faceted, which gives them their lovely, light-reflective quality.

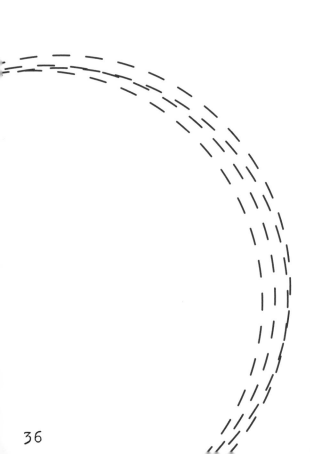

Seed beads come in a range of colors and finishes, from matte to iridescent, and in a number of shapes, from delicas (squared cylinders) to bugle (thin, hollow tubes). Seed beads have their own sizing system—for example 6°, 7°, 8°, and so on. The higher the number, the smaller the bead.

You can purchase vintage beads separately or you can remove them from old jewelry to recycle into new designs. Hunting for beads in second hand stores is fun and economical. It's also eco-friendly and can yield unique finds.

Button Up

Buttons come in an infinite variety. The two standard types of buttons are flat or sew-through buttons, which are attached through two or four holes, and shank buttons, which are attached through a loop on the back. Look for unique finds in vintage shops, at flea markets, and at charity shops. You might just end up collecting quite a stash.

Long Skinny Things

Choosing the right bead-stringing material is crucial to the success of your project. The heavier the jewelry, the stronger thread or wire you'll need.

Neck wires are shaped and pre-measured. They can be made of smooth or cable wire. Some come with a clasp already attached. Choose a metal that works with your jewelry design. Chain links of varying shapes and sizes provide numerous design possibilities.

Flexible beading wire has many brand names, but its basic structure is the same. It's made by bundling multi-strands of steel together, which are then coated in nylon to create a wire that is strong and flexible. Flexible beading wires are sold in different diameters with both clear and colored coatings.

Beading thread and cord can be made of polymid, synthetic fibers, cotton, or silk. Choose the size and type of thread most appropriate for the beads in your design.

Other decorative fiber options for stringing and constructing fabric jewelry pieces include ribbon, waxed linen, artificial sinew, leather, silk, hemp, and neoprene cords.

Francis Willemstijn
Brooch, Bye Bye My Miami Blue, 2008

13 x 8 x 3 cm

Silver, iron, velvet, wood

Photo by artist
Courtesy of Charon Kransen Arts, New York, NY

DESIGNER
Wendi Gratz

Button Down Bracelet

This is a great project for using the tiniest scraps of your most beautiful fabrics. Exercise your sense of design—using fabrics that work together beautifully—to create a bracelet you'll enjoy making and be proud to wear.

Try This

1. For each button, mark a fabric circle 1¾ inches (4.4 cm) in diameter. Cut a circle slightly larger than the marked circle with sharp scissors. It doesn't have to be perfect; a rough cut is fine (figure 1).

2. Wrap a fabric circle over the top rounded part of one button, hooking it under the teeth all the way around (figure 2).

{ Fig. 1 }

{ Fig. 2 }

3. Snap on the back half of the button to grab the fabric (figure 3).

4. Repeat steps 2 and 3 for the rest of the buttons, using a different fabric scrap for each.

5. Attach a crimp to one end of the rattail. Using a split ring, attach the clasp hook to the crimp (figure 4).

6. Tie a knot very close to the crimp. Thread the first button on the cord. Tie a second knot very close to the first knot to hold the button in place (figure 5).

7. Tie a third knot about ⅜ inch (1 cm) from the second knot. Add a second button to the cord and tie a knot on the other side.

8. Repeat step 7 to place the remaining five buttons on the rattail, each knotted in place.

9. Cut the cord about ½ inch (1.3 cm) from the last knot. Attach the second crimp to the cut end of the cord. Attach the clasp eye to the crimp.

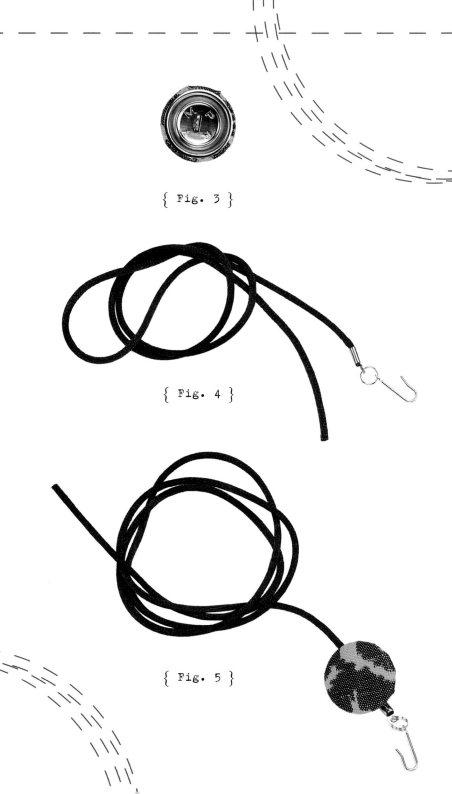

{ Fig. 3 }

{ Fig. 4 }

{ Fig. 5 }

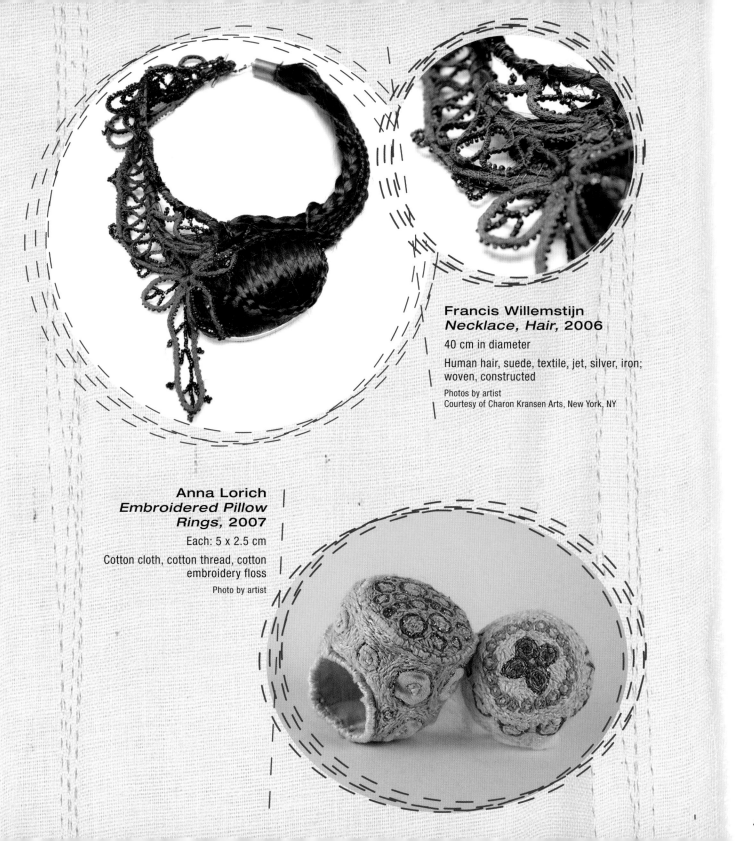

Francis Willemstijn
Necklace, Hair, 2006

40 cm in diameter

Human hair, suede, textile, jet, silver, iron;
woven, constructed

Photos by artist
Courtesy of Charon Kransen Arts, New York, NY

Anna Lorich
*Embroidered Pillow
Rings,* 2007

Each: 5 x 2.5 cm

Cotton cloth, cotton thread, cotton
embroidery floss

Photo by artist

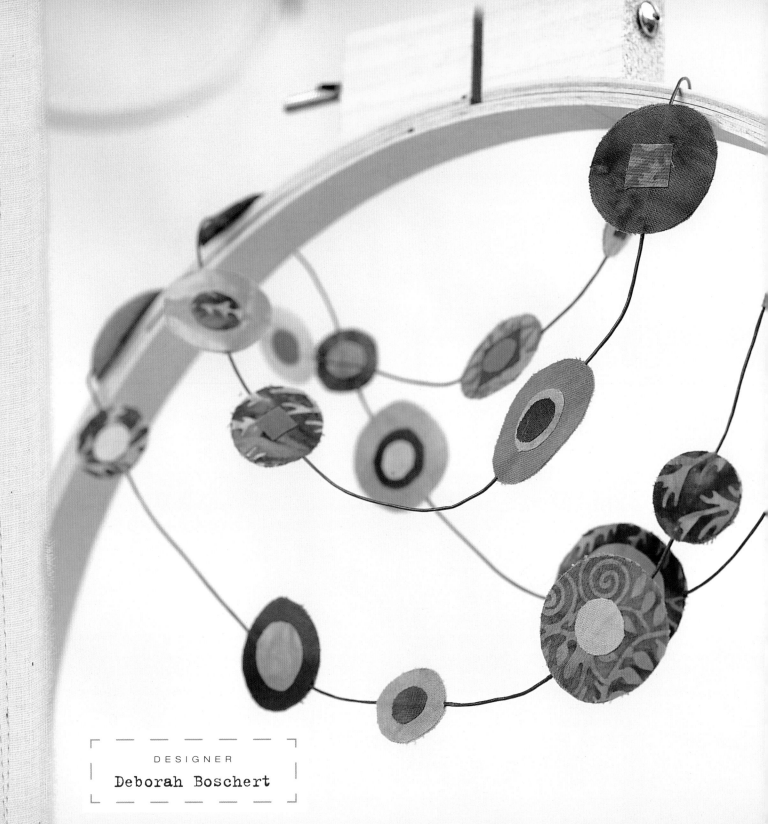

DESIGNER
Deborah Boschert

Circles and Circles and Squares (Oh My!)

This super simple necklace lends itself to any color palette or selection of shapes. The project shown uses many circles of blues and greens with just a few squares, which might remind you of that old adage: a square peg in a round hole.

Try This

1. Attach the fusible interfacing to the wrong side of each fabric square, following the manufacturer's instructions. Tear off the release paper.

2. Cut out sets of shapes using the measurements listed on the next page, or just wing it! A variety of shapes and fabrics give the necklace a dynamic look. Fold the fabric squares in half so you can cut two medium and two large circles at one time. Keep the matching pairs together (figure 1).

{ Fig. 1 }

Get This

5 solid-colored pieces of fabric, each 6 inches (15.2 cm) square

2 coordinating print pieces of fabric, each 6 inches (15.2 cm) square

Paper-backed fusible interfacing

48-inch (121.9 cm) faux leather cord, also in a coordinating color

Small scissors

Iron

TIP: Feel free to use fabrics from your stash, even if they're different sizes. The measurements here are just to get you started.

43

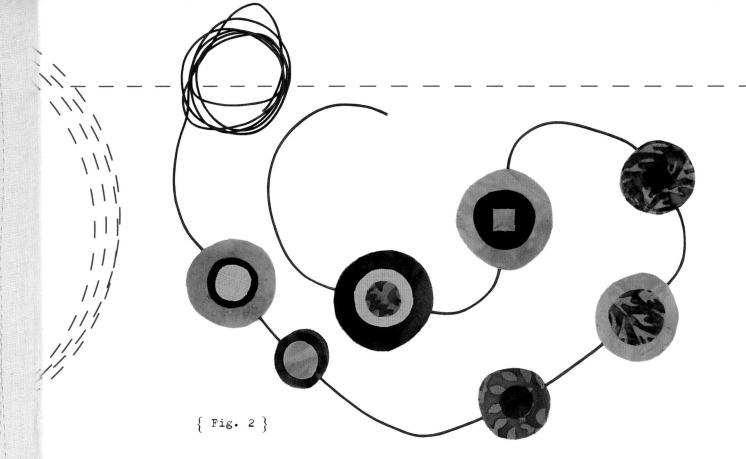

{ Fig. 2 }

- 6 matching pairs of large circles, 1 to 1¾ inches (2.5 to 4.4 cm) in diameter

- 10 matching pairs of medium circles, ½ to 1 inch (1.3 to 2.5 cm) in diameter

- 15 small circles, less than ½ inch (1.3 cm) in diameter

- 15 small squares, less than ½ inch (1.3 cm) in diameter

3. Lay out the cord on an ironing surface, and place the medium and large circles on top of it for placement ideas. Holding the cord taut between two fingers, center one pair of large circles, fusible sides together, over and under the cord. When the circles align, fuse them together.

4. Repeat step 3 to fuse the large and medium circles along the length of the cord, saving one pair to join the ends. Put some circles close together and others further apart, mixing up the sizes and fabrics (figure 2).

5. Close the necklace by carefully placing both ends of the cord between the last matching pair of circles. Fuse them together.

6. Add layers and details by fusing more circles and squares onto the base shapes. Create a small composition on both sides of each shape. They don't need to match. This necklace has no front or back. If it flips over, it still looks great.

Joanne Haywood
Oslo Brooches, 2007

Each: 5 x 5 x 0.5 cm

Felt, silver, embroidery; handmade

Photo by Alan Parkinson

Jessica Fitzgerald
Aves Abstract Brooch, 2006

4 x 6 x 0.5 cm

Silver, fabric; fabricated

Photo by artist

DESIGNER
Elizabeth Beeson

Floating Tulle Earrings

This playful project is simple, yet inspirational. The tulle creates a column of bold color as it floats on the silver pin. The result is a delightfully unique set of earrings that are both vibrant in color and kinetic.

Try This

1. Fold one square of fabric in half vertically and again horizontally. Repeat folding both ways again to create 16 layers. Pin the edges of the fabric to keep it folded and set it aside. Repeat with the other piece of fabric.

2. With the compass and scrap paper, draw two circle templates, ½ inch (1.3 cm) in diameter. Then draw two more circles that are slightly smaller than the first pair. Cut out each circle, poke a hole in the centers, and set them aside.

TIP: This project looks the boldest when you choose bright colors. The eye naturally blends the colors together to create an ethereal quality to the earrings.

Get This

10-inch (25.4 cm) square of tulle in two different colors

2 sterling silver headpins, 2⅜ inches (6.7 cm) long

2 rubber earring backs

Tape measure

Pencil

Compass

Piece of scrap paper

Scissors

Needle-nose and round-nose jewelry pliers

Straight pins

{ Fig. 1 }

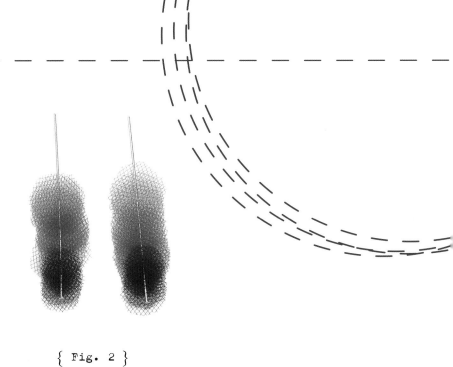

{ Fig. 2 }

3. Poke two silver headpins through one folded fabric square, leaving enough room all around both pins so the smaller templates will fit over the pins and not touch. Slide the smaller circle templates on the headpins so they rest against the fabric (figure 1).

4. Holding the fabric and templates together, carefully cut around the edges of each template until you have cut out a complete circle. Slide the template off the headpin to reveal 16 floating tulle discs on each headpin. Trim away any problem areas with the scissors.

5. Keep the tulle discs on the headpins. Repeat steps 3 and 4 with the second piece of folded fabric, except with the larger circle templates. The two head-pins should now have 16 small tulle discs at the bottom and 16 slightly larger tulle discs at the top (figure 2).

6. Slide the tulle to the bottom of one headpin. Using the needle-nose pliers, grip the headpin just above the fabric. A third of the way down toward the end of the headpin, bend the pin at a 45° angle with the jewelry pliers. Repeat with the second headpin.

7. Place the rubber earring backs on the end of each headpin. Lightly pinch the discs to cause them to float upwards on the silver pin. Enjoy!

TIP: You can create a dangling version of these earrings by looping the ends of the headpins and then attaching them to earring hooks.

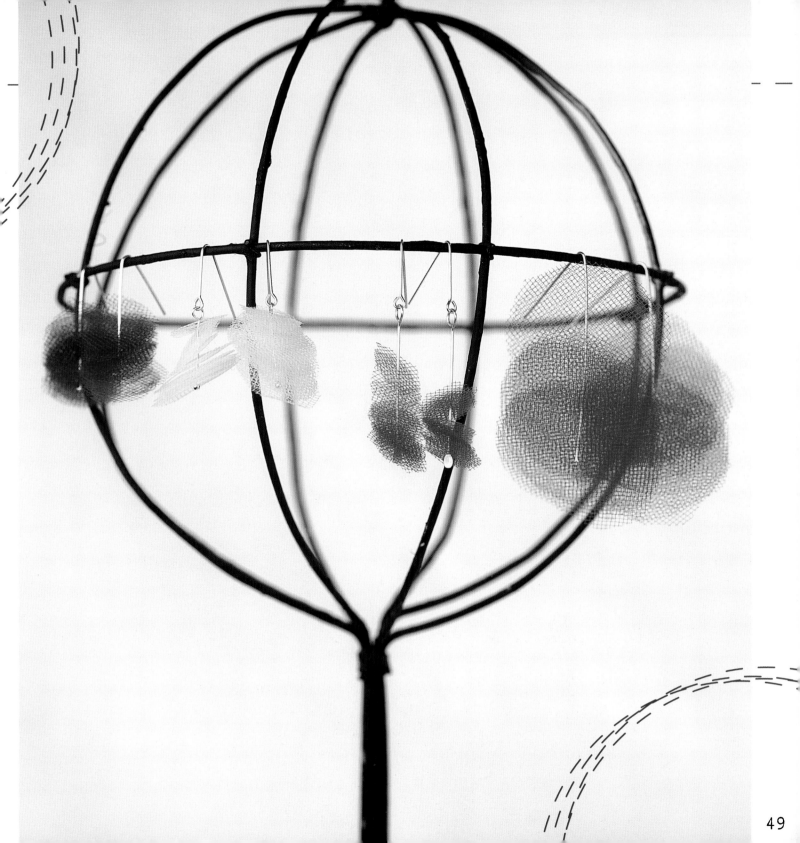

Spiro's
740 MARKET ST.
SAN FRANCISCO

DESIGNER
Mavis Leahy

Designer Label Brooch

Not everyone knows how versatile old clothing labels can be. It is simply amazing the different ways you can recycle them into brand-new accessories. This project uses them to create a whole new look. Visit your own closet—or a thrift shop—for some inspiration.

Get This

Clothing label

Belt buckle, slightly larger than the label

Two complementary scraps of fabric, 4 x 5 inches (10.2 x 12.7 cm)

Strip of lightweight fabric (silk, organdy, lace), ¼ x 30 inches (6 mm x 76.2 cm) Metallic embroidery thread

Lightweight cardboard, slightly larger than the belt buckle

Metal pin back

Button, seed beads, jewelry (optional)

Clear-drying craft glue

Straight pins

Needle

Scissors

Wire cutters

File

Fabric marker

Pencil

Books (or other flat, heavy objects)

Try This

1. Remove the center prong from the belt buckle with the wire cutters. File down the sharp ends of the buckle as needed. Dab craft glue on one end of the strip of lightweight fabric and adhere it to the buckle. Wrap the strip around the buckle until it's completely covered and then secure the end with more craft glue. Let it dry.

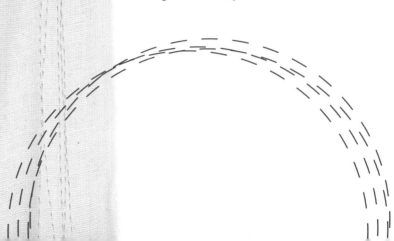

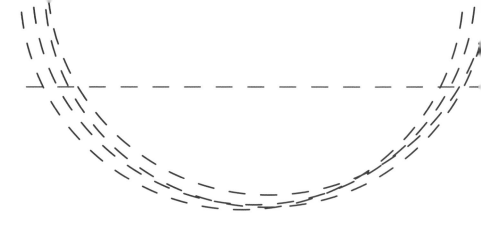

{ Fig. 1 }

{ Fig. 2 }

{ Fig. 3 }

{ Fig. 4 }

2. Wrap the fabric-covered buckle with metallic embroidery thread, using craft glue to secure the ends (figure 1). Let it dry.

3. Set the wrapped buckle on one of the 4 x 5-inch (10.2 x 12.7 cm) scraps of fabric, right side up. Trace the outside edge of the buckle onto the fabric with the marker. Center and pin the label in the middle of the fabric. Using the metallic embroidery thread, sew the pinned label onto the fabric with a simple whipstitch— or for the adventurous, use a decorative buttonhole stitch (figure 2). Following the outline, cut the fabric to the wrapped buckle's shape.

4. Center the buckle on the piece of cardboard and trace the outside edge in pencil. Cut ⅛ inch (3 mm) inside the line, so the cardboard is slightly smaller than the buckle. Coat the cardboard with a thin layer of glue. Center the other scrap of fabric, right side up, over the cardboard. Glue it down and let it dry (figure 3). Using the scissors, cut the fabric ½ inch (1.3 cm) larger than the cardboard all the way around. Clip the edges and fold the fabric over the cardboard to the other side (figure 4).

5. With the fabric-covered side of the cardboard face down, spread a thin layer of craft glue on the top, uncovered side. Adhere the fabric with sewn label, right side up. Put the fabric and cardboard under weight—books work well—and let the glue set.

{ Fig. 5 }

6. Coat the underside of the buckle with glue and set it on top of the fabric-covered cardboard, label side up. Place weight, like the books, on top again and let the glue set.

7. If you decide to embellish your brooch, glue the buttons, beads, or jewelry to the fabric-wrapped buckle (figure 5).

8. Center the pin back on back of brooch. Err toward the top of the brooch. Glue it down and let it dry (figure 6).

{ Fig. 6 }

DESIGNER
Steven James

Chrysalis Neckpiece

The remnants of a butterfly's abandoned cocoon inspired this piece. The black pods look like nature's work, yet it's a simple technique to reproduce. For different looks, consider alternative thread colors.

Try This

1. To make one pod, inflate one balloon to 1½ to 2 inches (3.8 to 5.1 cm) and tie it off. Then cut 25 pieces of thread 10 to 12 inches (25.4 to 30.5 cm) in length (figure 1).

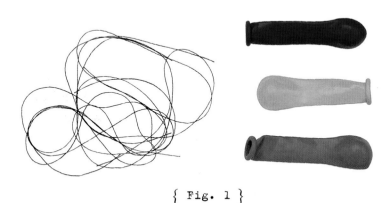

{ Fig. 1 }

Get This

Fabric stiffener

Spool of black 100% cotton thread

Black silk, nylon or cotton cord, 6 feet (1.8 m) in length

2 silver clamshell end tips

2 silver jump rings

Lobster claw clasp

Clear nail polish

Low-odor spray sealant (optional)

Small pushpin

5 latex water balloons, one per pod

Small plastic or glass bowl

Small pair of sharp scissors and tweezers

Craft wire (optional)

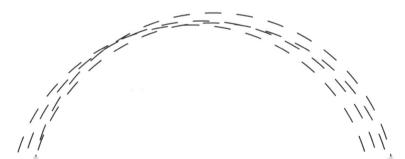

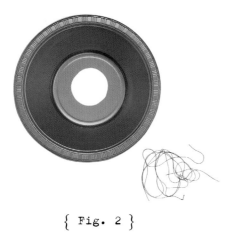

{ Fig. 2 }

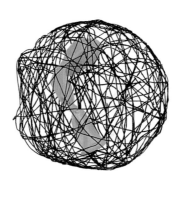

{ Fig. 3 }

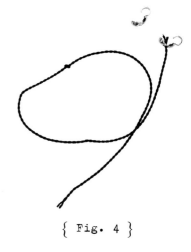

{ Fig. 4 }

2. Pour one tablespoon of fabric stiffener into the small bowl. Working over a protected surface, dip the thread, one piece at a time into the bowl and draw it through your fingers to apply the stiffener. Repeat until the thread is coated sufficiently, but not dripping or beading with stiffener (figure 2).

3. Gently wrap the coated thread around the balloon, making sure to overlap the ends. As you place the thread, draw it through your fingers to remove excess stiffener. While the first thread is drying, prepare the next thread. Continue to overlap pieces until the balloon is adequately covered. To prevent the stiffener from building up on your fingers, periodically wash them under running water.

4. Set the balloon aside and allow it to dry for several hours. Then use the pin to puncture the balloon (figure 3). Carefully remove the balloon from inside the webbing with the tweezers. You can remove any excess stiffener from the threads, but they add to the organic look of the piece, so consider keeping them in place.

5. Repeat steps 1 through 4 for each of pods, adding fabric stiffener to the bowl as needed. Consider making extra pods, in case some don't turn out well. Optionally, string the pods onto the craft wire and spritz them with low-odor spray sealant to give the thread a little more shine. Allow them to dry before continuing.

— — — — — — —

TIP: Keep in mind that the pods, while stiff, are still susceptible to firm pressure, so use caution when working with them and when wearing the necklace.

— — — — — — —

6. To suspend the pods from the cord, you can use additional pieces of thread or 26-gauge sterling silver wire (for a more elegant look). Starting in the center of the necklace, firmly double-knot (or wrap the wire) to secure the first pod into place (figure 4). Measure 1 inch (2.5 cm) in each direction and repeat. Continue to attach all five pods to the cord. For a more finished look, consider adding small, knotted thread pieces between each pod.

TIP: For a more organic feel, dangle the pods at slightly different lengths. As long as the pods are secure, you can attach them to the cord any way you wish.

7. Secure the end tips to the cord by tying a double knot 1 inch (2.5 cm) from each end of the cord. Apply a coat of clear nail polish over the knot and allow it to dry. Slide one end of the cord through the back of the end tip and then tie another double knot so it rests inside the tip (figure 4 again). Apply clear nail polish over the knot and allow it to dry. Gently close the tip shell over the knot and snip the excess cord. Repeat at the other end of the cord. Close the loops on the end tips and attach each part of the clasp to an end tip with the jump rings.

Åsa Halldin
Untitled, 2006

200 cm in length

Flax thread, organza flowers, metal thread; wound, stitched

Photo by Adrian Nordenborg

DESIGNER
Miyuki Akai Cook

Kaga Earrings

Old fabric becomes new jewelry. This project uses vintage kimono silk from Kaga, Japan's renowned region for textile production. Making the earrings gives you an ingenious and elegant way to recycle.

Try This

1. Cut a ¾-inch (1.9 cm) wide x 3½ inches (8.9 cm) long bias strip from your fabric (figure 1). Cut a ¹⁄₁₆-inch (5 mm) wide x 3½ inches (8.9 cm) long rice paper strip.

2. On a short edge of the index card, measure and mark ¼ inch (6 mm) three times. Cut along the markings so you have three strips and tape them together to create one longer strip.

3. Fold ⅛ inch (3 mm) at one end of the bias strip and wrap it, right side down, around the glue stick. Cut off the excess fabric.

{ Fig. 1 }

Get This

- Vintage Japanese fabric (or any silky fabric), 7 x 7 inches (17.8 x 17.8 cm)
- Rice paper, ¼ x 7 inches (6 mm x 17.8 cm)
- Index card
- Rayon embroidery floss in two complementary colors (e.g., red and white)
- Pair of earring hooks
- 2 flat headpins
- 2 sewing needles
- Straight pin
- Scissors
- Ruler (metric measurements are preferred)
- Calculator
- Fine-tip red pen
- Transparent cellophane tape
- Glue stick
- Round-nose pliers
- Wire cutters

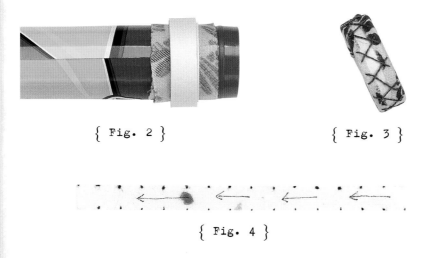

{ Fig. 2 }　　　　　　{ Fig. 3 }

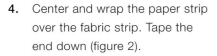

{ Fig. 4 }

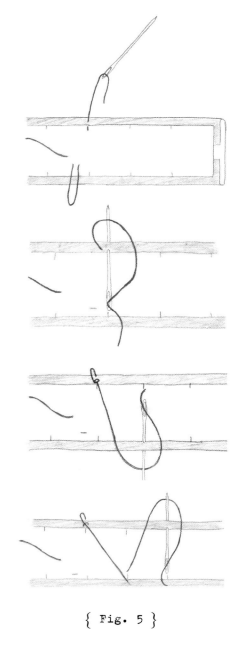

{ Fig. 5 }

4. Center and wrap the paper strip over the fabric strip. Tape the end down (figure 2).

5. Fold both sides of the fabric around the paper ring and stitch it down (figure 3).

6. Wrap the rice paper around the ring to measure its length around. Cut it to the exact same length as the ring. Measure the rice paper and divide its length by 15. Use a metric ruler, if possible, and the calculator. Accuracy is important. Use the pen to mark the paper (figure 4).

7. Draw arrows on the paper in one direction to indicate the direction to stitch. Also draw one dot with the pen for the starting point

(figure 4 again). When you're done, wrap the rice paper around the ring, securing it with the tape.

8. Poke the pin through the ring to create a hole for the flat headpin. Push the headpin through the hole from inside of the ring to the outside.

9. Thread one sewing needle with the first color of embroidery floss. (I used red.) Do not make a knot. Stitch into the ring toward the edge of the marked starting point. Stitch out near the opposite edge. Stitch in close to the point where you came out and stitch out at the starting point on the opposite edge of the ring (figure 5).

10. Always stitch along the edges of the ring, except for when you start and end. Loop stitch at the first mark. Following the arrows for direction, loop stitch at the second mark. Continue until the stitch comes back to the starting point. You've finished the first circle. Stitch one more circle (figure 6).

11. Keeping the first floss on the needle, thread the other color of embroidery floss on the second needle (I used white). Stitch one circle. Meanwhile the first needle and floss remains near the ending point (figure 7).

12. Switch needles. Lay the white floss aside, and stitch two circles with the red floss. Alternate between the colors—one circle in white and two in red—until you've completely filled the ring with stitches.

13. With the round-nose pliers, create a wire loop in the headpin as close to the ring as possible. Wrap the wire end around the neck of the loop and cut off the excess. Attach an earring hook.

14. Repeat to create a matching earring.

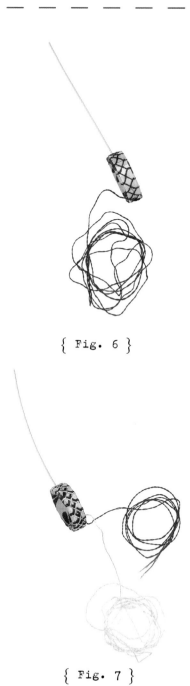

{ Fig. 6 }

{ Fig. 7 }

Miyuki Akai Cook
Kaga Necklace 1, 2006

23 x 16 x 2 cm

Paper, rice paper, silver, Japanese vintage fabric, rayon thread; stitched

Photos by artist
Courtesy of Mobilia Gallery, Cambridge, MA

Fully Felt Wristlet

This fun, fanciful felt bracelet will fill your day with funky goodness! It will also warm your wrist and the cockles of your heart. It's so easy to make, you can whip up a bunch for yourself and your friends.

Get This

- Graph paper with ¼-inch (6 mm) grid
- Three 9 x 12-inch (22.9 x 30.5 cm) sheets of craft felt in coordinating colors
- Cardboard or card stock
- ½-inch (1.3 cm) masking or invisible tape
- Sewing thread
- Two ⅜-inch (1 cm) snaps
- Pencil
- Ruler
- Straight pins
- Scissors
- Sewing machine (optional)
- Hand-sewing needle
- 2 spools of thread in variegated colors: lavender/purple and yellow/gold
- Heat-and-bond light fusing
- 5 strands of yarn, any variety, each about 34 inches (86.4 cm) in length
- Sewing machine
- Sharp fabric scissors

Try This

1. Using the template on page 140 or the tip below as a guide, create a pattern for the felt shapes on the graph paper. (You can also use card stock or cardboard to make the pattern.) For an accurate transfer, plot the end points and draw it with the ruler. Pin the pattern to the felt and cut out seven pieces of each color.

TIP: After you get comfortable with this technique, try some shapes and patterns of your own. You can dramatically change the look of the wristlet by changing the felt shapes.

2. Measure 8 inches (20.3 cm) on the piece of cardboard or card stock and attach a piece of the tape with sticky side up on those 8 inches (20.3 cm). Space each cut felt piece evenly along the tape, keeping each piece centered on the tape and mixing the colors (figure 1). They should cover the entire 8 inches, which will create a bracelet that fits an average-sized arm. Adjust the size of the tape or the placement of the felt pieces, if necessary. When satisfied, center another piece of tape over the top of the felt for added security (figure 2).

3. Remove the felt from the cardboard. Cut two 1 x 10-inch (2.5 x 25.4 cm) pieces of felt in the trim color of your choice. Sandwich the strip of taped felt pieces between the two lengths of trim felt. Leave a ¼-inch (6 mm) tail at the first end of the taped strip, so the long end of the felt tail is at the other end.

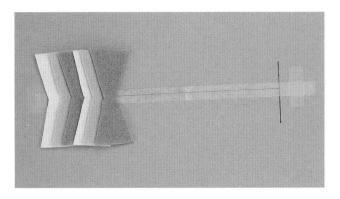

{ Fig. 1 }

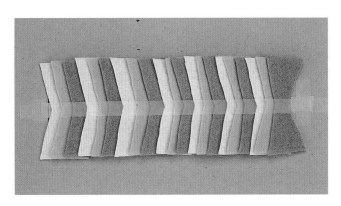

{ Fig. 2 }

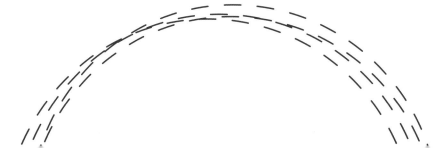

4. Pin the three sections together in the middle, making sure they are centered and aligned on both sides. Allowing for a ¼-inch (6 mm) seam allowance, stitch along the length of one side. Remove the pins and the tape. Then sew the other side and the ends in the same manner.

5. Using a buttonhole stitch, attach the first female snap to the long end of the tail very close to the end. Attach the second one approximately 1¼ inches (3.2 cm) down, from snap center to snap center. On the opposite side of the bracelet, place the first male snap at the point where the first shape emerges from the trim. Measure 1¼ inches (3.2 cm) down, from snap center to snap center, and sew on the second male snap.

TIP: The color pattern of the bracelet will flow without interruption if you place the snaps correctly.

DESIGNER
Andrea L. Stern

Lotus Choker & Earrings

This serene lotus flower, with its velvet choker, is part Southern belle and part Eastern mystique. The cute matching dangle earrings look like exotic blossoms from the Orient. It's jewelry fusion at its finest.

CHOKER

Try This

1. Measure your neck. Subtract 1 inch (2.5 cm) to allow for the clasp and cut the ribbon to that length. (Your clasp might be a different size; check before cutting.) Attach the split rings to the ribbon crimps, and then crimp each end of the ribbon. Attach one half of the clasp to each split ring.

Get This

- ⅝-inch (1.6 cm) wide velvet ribbon in desired color, 18 inches (45.7 cm) long
- Leaf clasp
- 2 6-mm split rings, matching the clasp color
- 2 ribbon crimp ends
- ¼ yard (22.9 cm) of a flower-colored cotton fabric (one fat quarter)
- ¼ yard (22.9 cm) of batting (one fat quarter)
- Fabric marking pen
- Water-soluble interfacing
- Hand towel
- 14 crystal bicone beads, 5 mm
- 14 seed beads, 11° or smaller
- Wool serger thread or wool felt for stamen
- Tube turning tool or dull pencil
- Flat-nose pliers
- Scissors
- Hand-sewing needle
- Sewing machine
- Embroidery threads
- Machine embroidery hoop
- Measuring tape
- Straight pins

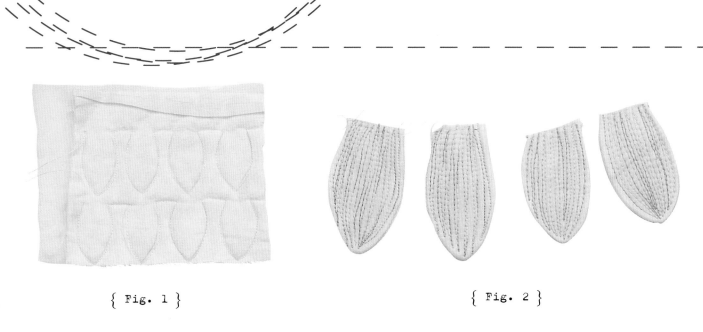

{ Fig. 1 }

{ Fig. 2 }

2. Fold the fabric with right sides together and pin it to the batting. Draw 10 to 12 (or as many as you want) petal shapes on the fabric, leaving at least ⅛-inch (3 mm) between them. Also draw one circular shape about the same size and set it aside until step 6. Stitch the layers together, leaving the bottom of each shape unstitched (figure 1).

3. Trim the petals ⅛-inch (3 mm) from the stitching and turn them right side out, using the tube turning tool or a dull pencil. Lay a piece of the interfacing on your machine embroidery hoop and place the petals in the ring. Cover it with a second piece of interfacing, and secure the hoop to your sewing machine. Lower

the feed dogs and with a variegated or colored thread, machine embroider the veins of the petals onto each petal. Repeat until you've embroidered all the petals (figure 2).

4. Remove the hoop and trim away the excess interfacing. Dissolve the remaining interfacing by pouring very hot water in a bowl over the petals and swirling them through the water. Rinse them with cool water if desired, but do not let them soak. Lay the petals on a towel to dry.

5. Make the stamens from a circle of wool felt as in step 8 or as follows. Stretch a piece of interfacing in the machine embroidery hoop. Wind the bobbin of your sewing machine with the wool serger thread in a color that complements the petals. Zigzag stitch a 1- to 1½-inch (2.5 to 3.8 cm) circular shape onto the interfacing. Sew the same shape two to three times, trim the thread ends, and dissolve the interfacing as in step 4, except do not rinse the stamens. Let them dry.

{ Fig. 3 }

{ Fig. 4 }

6. Stitch the circular shape you made in step 2 in one of two ways. Either sew the entire circle and then make a slash in the center of the fabric to turn the piece right side out (figure 3)—the petals will hide the slash—or leave part of the seam unstitched and turn it right side out through the opening.

7. When the petals are dry, pin five or six of them in concentric circles to form a base. Hand sew or machine stitch very slowly, one petal at a time until they are all attached. Tie off and knot the thread. Then layer another level of five or six petals inside the first, leaving just a bit of the base showing (figure 4). Tie off and knot the thread.

8. Sew the stamens that you made in step 5 into the center of the flower, fluffing them as you stitch (figure 4 again). Alternatively, cut a 1½- to 2-inch (3.8 to 5.1 cm) circle of wool felt and cut into it around the edges to make fringe. Then sew the wool into the center of the flower.

9. Sew the crystal beads into the center of the flower, pairing each with a seed bead. Whipstitch the base of the flower to the center of the ribbon.

EARRINGS

Get This

2 headpins, 3 inches (7.6 cm) in length

Pair of earring hooks

Crimping tool

4 scrapbook eyelets

Eyelet setter

Hole punch

Wire cutters

26-gauge base metal or sterling silver wire, 12 inches (30.5 cm) in length

Scrap of fabric from the choker, about 5 inches (12.7 cm) square

Scrap of green fabric for the leaf, about 5 inches (12.7 cm) square

Fusible interfacing

4 crystal bicone beads, 5 mm

2 glass beads, 3 mm

4 glass beads, 6 mm

2 glass beads, 8 mm

4 gold-filled round beads, 2 mm

Round-nose pliers

Scissors

Hand-sewing needle

Sewing machine

Embroidery threads

Machine embroidery hoop

Measuring tape

Straight pins

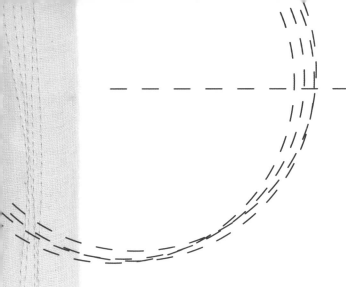

Try This

1. Draw four flower shapes and four leaf shapes, each about 2½ inches (5.7 cm) in diameter on the paper side of the fusible interfacing. Fuse the shapes to the wrong side of the respective fabrics (that is, green for the leaf shape). Trim the shapes and peel off the backing paper. Fold the fabric with right sides together and pin it to the batting. Draw 10 to 12 (or as many as you want) petal shapes on the fabric, leaving at least ⅛-inch (3 mm) between them. Also draw one circular shape about the same size and set it aside until step 6. Stitch the layers together, leaving the bottom of each shape unstitched.

2. Repeat step 1, but don't trim the shapes. Put the wrong sides of the matching fabric pieces together.

3. Set your machine for a narrow zigzag stitch and use thread colors that match the fabric for the needle and bobbin. Stitch along the edges of the flower petals. Fill in the petal veins with machine embroidery. Repeat the narrow zigzag stitching with green thread for the edges of the leaves, but run a piece of the wire along the edge as you stitch. Go slowly and trap the wire under the stitches. Trim the wire edges closely. Use a crimping tool to smooth them if necessary. Fill in the leaf veins with machine embroidery.

4. Trim the flowers and leaves, being careful not to cut into the stitching. If necessary, apply a little fray check to catch any loose threads.

5. Using the hole punch, make holes in the center of the petal and leaf shapes. Set an eyelet in each hole using the eyelet setting tool. Shape the leaf slightly by pinching the petals toward the center.

6. String each earring onto a head-pin as follows: 3-mm glass bead, crystal bead, 6-mm glass bead, flower petal (right side out), 8-mm glass bead, leaf (right side out, 6-mm glass bead, 2-mm gold-filled bead, crystal bead, 2-mm gold-filled bead

7. Bend the headpin at a 90° angle at the top. Trim it to ¼ inch (6 mm) from the bend, and then make a loop using the pliers. Attach the earring hooks to the loop.

Dianne Frank
Once Removed #1, 2007

43.2 x 35.6 cm

Antique appliqué, bronze, embroidery
floss, antique costume pearls

Photos by Darrell Appelzdler

DESIGNER

**Sarah Terry of
Guerilla Embroidery, UK**

Stitched and Stuffed Necklace

Is this pendant a pillow, a plush toy, or a multidimensional work of art? Whatever you call it, you're sure to enjoy creating this unique piece that combines traditional and reverse appliqués, contrasting fabrics, ribbons, and a button.

Get This

- 3 fabric pieces, 6 inches (15.2 cm) square
- Paper pattern cut into desired pendant shape
- Contrasting fabric piece, 4 inches (10.2 cm) square
- Matching thread
- Scrap of wool or acrylic felt, 2 inches (5.1 cm) square
- 4 matching ribbons, each 1 inch (2.5 cm) long
- Small button
- Polyester wadding

- Jewelry pliers
- Fabric scissors
- Sewing machine
- Darning presser foot
- Hand-sewing needle
- Fabric-marking pen or pencil
- Straight pins
- Iron
- 3 jump rings
- Neck cable of your choice
- Clasp to match

Try This

Making the Pendant

1. Pin two 6-inch (15.2 cm) fabric squares with right sides together.

2. Design your pendant shape on paper. With the fabric pen or pencil, trace the pendant shape onto the wrong side of the top fabric piece, using the paper pattern as a guide. Within the drawn shape, sketch another circular shape on the fabric. This shape doesn't need to be perfect; sometimes it looks better if it isn't!

{ Fig. 1 }

{ Fig. 2 }

3. Drop the feed dogs on your sewing machine and replace the regular straight stitch presser foot with the darning foot. Check your manual for instructions, if necessary. Stitch around the inner circle, at least two times for extra strength. Then cut out the inner circle, about 1/32 inch (1 mm) inside the stitches.

4. Remove the pins and turn the fabric through the hole from front to back. Press it with an iron on a steam setting until it's flat on both sides. You may need to work the fabric with your fingers to get it to lie flat properly (figure 1). Choose one fabric to be the front and the other to be the lining.

5. Pin the 4-inch (10.2 cm) square contrasting fabric to the lining fabric, so that the right side is visible through the hole. Sew it in place by stitching around the hole. Flip the piece over and trim off the excess fabric. On the front of the piece, lightly trace around the pendant pattern so you embellish that area only (figure 2).

6. Change the thread to match the color of the felt. Cut the felt into two rounded petal shapes, and then cut out the middle of each. Position them next to the facing, fanning out from its edges. Sew once around the edge of each petal and then again 1/16 inch (1.6 mm) inside the first stitch.

7. Thread the hand-sewing needle. Decide where to place the button in the design and then sew it securely in place.

8. Pin the right side of the piece—the one you've been working on—to the right side of the last 6-inch (15.2 cm) square piece. Mark the shape of the pendant, remembering to add extra fabric for the seam allowance.

{ Fig. 3 }

9. Sew along the pendant marking. Backstitch at the beginning of the seam to make it extra secure. When you reach the point where you want the first ribbon loop, place it between the two pieces of fabric, with the loop facing inside the pendant, and sew right over the ends to catch them in the seam. Repeat with the other three ribbons. Sew all the way around the pendant, leaving a 1-inch (2.5 cm) opening so you can turn the pendant right side out. Backstitch at the end of your sewing to stop the fabric tearing when you turn it.

10. Trim off any excess fabric, leaving a ¼-inch (6 mm) seam allowance. Turn the pendant inside out. Stuff the pendant with the wadding until the pendant is firm to the touch. Fold the fabric at the opening to the inside of the pendant and hand-sew it closed. Use a slipstitch or the smallest possible running stitch (figure 3).

Making the Necklace

11. Sew one of the jump rings onto the top of the pendant, behind the seam. Secure it well with several stitches.

12. To complete the necklace, thread one end of the neck cable through the jump ring until the pendant is opposite the cable's fastening.

DESIGNER
Ellen Gerritse

Swing Set

In these artful earrings, color, pattern, and texture merge into a captivating fabric collage. Slim silver wires hold the abstracted leaf forms. As a bonus, the instructions tell you how to make two pairs of earrings—one to wear and one to share.

Get This

- 6 pieces of thin fabric in matching colors, each 11¾ inches (30 cm) square
- Acrylic fortifier (available in DIY stores)
- Plate or small container
- Wax baking paper
- Silver marker with a thin tip
- 20-gauge sterling silver wire, 44 inches (112 cm) in length
- 8 sterling silver cones (or bead caps)
- 8 seed beads, color coordinated with the fabric
- 8 20-gauge sterling silver headpins, 3 inches (7.6 cm) in length
- All purpose glue
- Scissors
- Round-nose pliers
- Wire cutters
- Hammer
- Clothespins

TIP: Be sure to include tulle as one of the fabrics, as well as one or two fabrics with a small print motif.

Try This

1. Cut about 100 leaf shapes in various sizes, none larger than 2 inches (5.1 cm). Cut different sizes from each of the fabrics so you get a good mix (figure 1).

{ Fig. 1 }

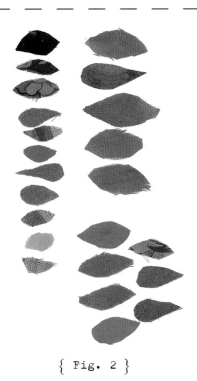

{ Fig. 2 }

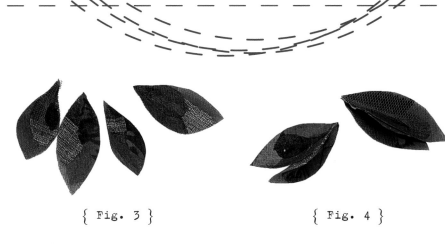

{ Fig. 3 }   { Fig. 4 }

2. Sort the leaves into four groups of the same approximate size (figure 2).

3. Mix and match the fabric leaves, taking one from each size group, to create 24 stacks with four leaves each. Stack the leaves from largest to smallest, with the largest leaf on the bottom.

TIP: It doesn't matter if any of the fabric leaves have frayed ends. The acrylic fortifier will stop the fraying, and the frays will blend within the layers.

4. Cut a large piece of the wax paper and place it on a flat surface. Pour some of the acrylic fortifier on a plate or in a small container. One at a time, dip each of the 24 stacks of leaves into the fortifier and arrange them on the wax paper. Let them dry overnight.

5. Once dry, the leaves in each stack should be stuck together, hardened but still flexible (figure 3). Create dotted designs on some of the leaves with the silver marker.

6. Vertically pinch the base of each stack to add contour. Then, glue two stacks together so that the edges of the leaves align (see the project photo). Hold them together with clothespins. Repeat with the remaining stacks, so you have 12 pairs of folded leaf stacks, glued together (figure 4). Let them dry.

7. While the leaves are drying, cut 16 pieces of the silver wire: eight 3⅜ inches (7.9 cm) long and eight 2⅜-inches (6 cm) long. Hammer flat one end of each wire.

8. Apply glue near the top of one long wire and stick it through the fold at the base of one leaf stack until it extends approximately ¼ inch (6 mm) above the leaf. Fold the base of the stack around the wire. Hold it closed to set the glue. Repeat with a short wire into the other stack of the same pair.

9. Dab a drop of glue inside one of the silver cones or caps and string it onto a leaf stack pair so that the end of the wire sticks out. Push the cone down as far as you can; it will hold the fabric and the wire together.

10. Repeat steps 8 and 9 for the seven remaining joined leaf stacks, using the other 14 pieces of cut wire and the other seven cones. Give the glue time to dry completely.

11. Bend the wire that sticks out of the top of each cone into a small loop, using the round-nose pliers. Trim any excess wire. Bend each headpin at the following points from the blunt end, in the same direction: ⅝ inch (1.6 cm) and 1½ inch (3.8 cm). Using the round-nose pliers again, gently curve each leg of the wire as shown in the project photo.

12. Hook the loops of two leaf stacks so that they sit back-to-back on the wire at the first bend. Add one of the seed beads. Reshape any of the wires as desired so the earring hangs evenly. Repeat to create three other earrings.

Lisa Björke
I'm All Ears, **2006**
40 x 30 x 3 cm
Wool felt; machine embroidered
Photo by artist

79

DESIGNER
Anika Smulovitz

Jellyfish Pendant

Global warming over the past few years has resulted in a subtle increase of ocean temperatures, which in turn has resulted in a measurable increase in jellyfish populations. Recycle old clothes as you create this visual reminder of the need to reduce consumer waste.

Get This

Thrift store clothes to deconstruct for parts

Hot glue gun and glue sticks

Metal hemisphere form, to cast hot glue (see Tip)

Silicone release spray (optional)

Sewing needle

Thread to match clothes

Razor blade

Scissors

TIP: The metal hemisphere form can be a tiny metal bowl, an inexpensive aluminum paint palette (figure 1), or a jeweler's dapping block (if you happen to have one in your studio).

{ Fig. 1 }

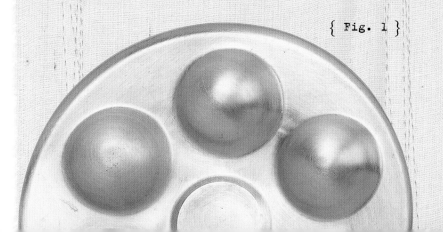

Try This

1. Once you have the right clothes (see Finding the Right Clothes, page 82), you can deconstruct them for parts. Remove ruffles and ribbons with a dull razor blade; carefully cut the thread that holds them to the garment (figure 2). Remove fringe from clothing with scissors. Mark the cut ends so you can place them into the hot glue form; otherwise, they might fray.

{ Fig. 2 }

Finding the Right Clothes

Before you start the project, rummage through thrift stores for clothes in poor condition or in really, really bad taste. Look for details that would work for the tentacles, feeding arms, and hanging ribbon. Shirts, skirts, or shawls with long fringe, ribbons, or ties make great tentacles (figure 3). Blouses, shirts, skirts, or dresses with small ruffles work for the feeding arms (figure 4). To hang your jellyfish pendant, use ribbon or ties, a strip of cloth from deconstructed clothing, or a homemade tie or ribbon.

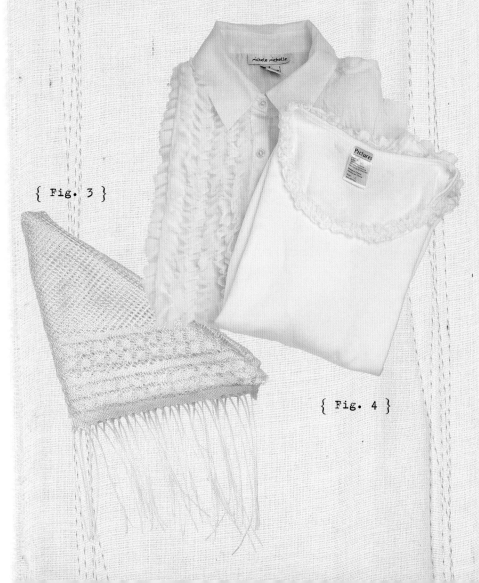

{ Fig. 3 }

{ Fig. 4 }

2. Cast the jellyfish body with the hot glue gun. Have extra glue sticks on hand. Use one of the following techniques, but do not fill the entire form with glue. You just need to create the outside layer in this step.

- Create a plaster mold of half of a small ball, about 1 inch (2.5 cm) in diameter. After the mold dries, soak the mold in water for one hour, which allows you to cast the glue right in the plaster without fear of the glue adhering.

- Cast the glue directly into the metal form without a release agent. Quickly coat the form with a layer of hot glue, from bottom to top. Before the glue cools completely, pull and tug the cast out of the mold. If you don't act quickly enough, the form will stick to the mold ... permanently.

- Before casting the glue into the metal form, spray the form with a silicone release spray. Spray with adequate ventilation, or outdoors, and read the label for the manufacturer's instructions and safety warnings. With the silicone barrier

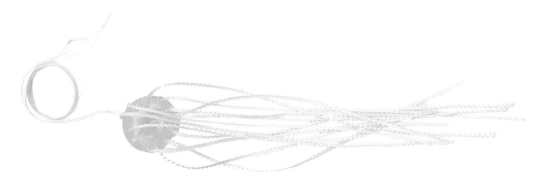

{ Fig. 5 }   { Fig. 6 }

in place, layer hot glue into the form, from the bottom to the top. Wait until the glue has cooled completely, and the cast should come out easily. Wash the silicone off the form with soap and water.

3. Using the needle and thread, sew through the center of the jellyfish body, leaving excess thread at of the top of the body to attach the hanging ribbon (figure 5).

4. Decide which clothing parts to use for tentacles and feeding arms. See the project photo for the length relationships between them. Slowly glue the tentacles to the interior edge of the jellyfish body with the glue gun (figure 6). Keep the metal form nearby

in case the jellyfish body starts to warp, in which case, put the body back into the form and let it cool. If you produce some glue strings, let them cool so you can pull them off.

5. Add four feeding arms by folding a ruffle in half and gluing the folded end in the center of the jellyfish body. Repeat to create the second two feeding arms. To avoid warping, keep the jellyfish body in the metal form as you glue. This also keeps the tentacles out of the way. If necessary, fill in the form with more glue. You'll want to keep the bottom of the form somewhat concave. In other words, the bottom does not have to be smooth, but it should definitely not be bulbous.

6. After the body cools, sew on the hanging ribbon. Also, wrap thread around the ends of the ruffles, or feeding arms, and sew them closed to make them look finished. Do the same to the ends of the hanging ribbon ties.

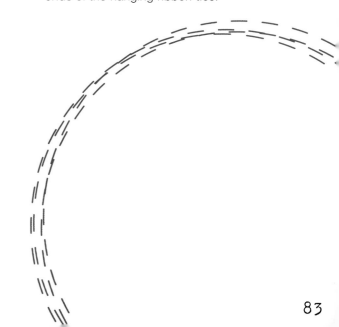

DESIGNER
Sara Gallo-Cornell

Frayed Fabric Bead Bracelet

You can manipulate a fabric's surface in many ways, from embellishing (building up) to fraying (wearing down). With this bracelet, you can see the results of the same technique on different fabrics. Vary the type, size, and surface treatment of each piece to make an infinite range of styles.

Try This

1. Lay the fabric square on a flat surface. Cut the fabric into 6 x 4-inch (15.2 x 10.2 cm) rectangles using fabric scissors to prevent the edges from fraying. Each rectangle will become a bead later on, so cut as many as you think you'll need.

TIP: You can distress all the beads, a few of them, half of them, or none of them. Experiment with different looks!

Get This

Silky fabric of your choice, 2 x 2 feet (61 x 61 cm)

Fabric scissors

Household scissors

Seam ripper (optional)

Sewing needle and matching thread

Embroidery floss

¾-inch-wide (1.9 cm) ribbon (optional)

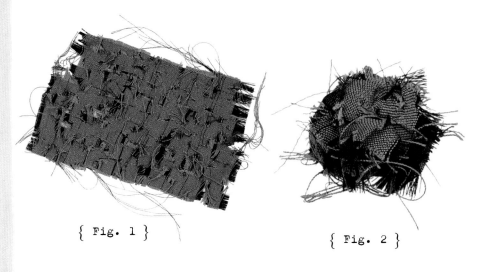

{ Fig. 1 }

{ Fig. 2 }

Slip-on or Clasp?

Optionally, you can make a fabric clasp for the bracelet instead of making a complete circle of beads. Cut two pieces of the ribbon, each 5 to 6 inches (12.7 to 15.2 cm) long. Sew one onto each side of the string of beads. Tie them together in a bow to hold the bracelet together.

2. To make a frayed fabric bead, use the seam ripper or household scissors to tear the surface of the fabric (figure 1). This adds lots of texture. You want as much fraying as possible, but take your time or it will look like a mess!

3. Thread the hand sewing needle and knot the thread. Lay each fabric rectangle (frayed and unfrayed) on a flat surface, right side down. Fold all four corners of one rectangle into the center, but do not press the fabric. Sew the corners down where you folded them. Repeat for every piece of fabric you cut.

4. Scrunch the center of one fabric rectangle between your thumb and fingers. Then fold and bunch up the rest of the fabric randomly to create volume. As you bunch, sew through the fabric, securing it into a rough ball shape. Continue bunching and sewing tightly to secure the ball. You may have to sew in and out five to ten times (figure 2).

5. Once you are satisfied with the shape of the bead, knot the thread and cut off the excess.

6. Repeat steps 4 and 5 with each fabric rectangle.

7. String the beads together with embroidery floss, which is thicker and more stable than thread. String one bead at a time, connecting them together with a secure knot. Use enough beads so that the bracelet slides over your wrist once the circle is complete. Once you have all the beads you want on the embroidery floss, connect the beginning and end bead and knot the floss. Cut away the excess.

Jennifer Halvorson
Laced Up, 2005

25.4 x 25.4 x 3.2 cm

Shoelaces, sewing thread, glue;
rolled, sewn

Photo by artist

Emily Gill
Floral Brooches, 2008

Each: 6 x 6.5 x 3 cm

Sterling silver, felt, cotton thread,
polyester filling; lost wax cast,
hand stitched

Photo by artist

Recycled Reward

Classic fabrics from men's clothing—houndstooth, herring-bone, or whatever you like—make for a classic necklace with a surprising twist. The beads in this project were crafted from fallen Australian timbers, but use whatever you can find, even non-wooden beads.

Get This

3 different fabric strips, 1 x 34 inches (2.5 x 86.4 cm)

6 wooden beads, each with a ¼-inch (6 mm) hole

Wooden bead in a toggle shape, 2 to 3 inches (5.1 to 7.6 cm) in length

19-gauge steel, sterling silver, or copper wire, 5 inches (12.7 cm) in length

26-gauge steel, sterling silver, or copper wire, 2 inches (5.1 cm) in length

Embroidery floss, color coordinated with fabric

Thread, color coordinated with fabric

Sewing machine

Scissors or rotary cutter with mat

Iron

Embroidery needle

Wire cutters

Pliers

Standard spool, without thread

Measuring tape

Try This

1. Iron the fabric to ensure precise measurements and cuts. Cut the fabric into strips 1 inch (2.5 cm) wide, in lengths of 32, 33, and 34 inches (81.3, 83.8, and 86.4 cm). A rotary cutter and mat make this easy, but you can also use a measuring tape and scissors.

TIP: If the repurposed fabric you have is not long enough, machine-stitch 1-inch (2.5 cm) strips together to obtain the desired lengths.

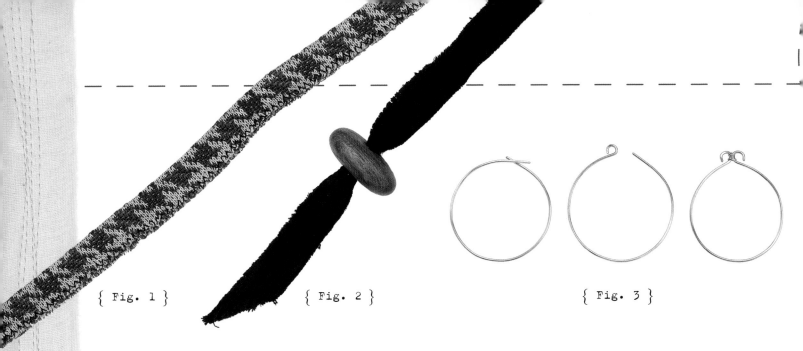

{ Fig. 1 }   { Fig. 2 }   { Fig. 3 }

2. Fold each strip in half lengthwise so the fabric edges meet evenly and press them with the iron. Select the temperature setting on the iron appropriate for the types of fabric.

3. Set your sewing machine for a narrow zigzag stitch. Stitch along the raw edges of the fabric strips to finish them and minimize raveling. If desired, use a contrasting thread color for a bolder looking finished product (figure 1).

4. Decide which fabric strip will hold the beads. A thick, durable fabric holds the beads the best. If you use a thin fabric, you may have to knot or glue the beads in place. Before stringing the beads, cut one end of the chosen strip into a point, which helps get the fabric through the bead hole (figure 2). Position the beads on the strip as desired. Leave ample space on each end to attach the other fabric strips and the clasp.

TIP: The beads you select need to have large enough holes to accommodate the fabric strips. If the fabric is bulky after it is sewn, you may need larger bead holes. If the fabric is sheer or thin, you may need beads with smaller holes.

5. Wrap the 5-inch (12.7 cm) length of wire around the standard spool. Form a loop on each end of the wire, facing in opposite directions (figure 3). Next, wrap the 2-inch (5.1 cm) wire through the loops to secure the circle.

6. Place the fabric strips on top of each other with the ends together. Place the wire circle 1 inch (2.5 cm) from one end and fold the strips over the wire. With the sewing machine, straight stitch the strips together. On the other end, fold the fabric over 1 inch (2.5 cm) from the end and machine-stitch them together.

7. Attach the toggle bead to the looped end of fabric with the needle and embroidery floss. To make a strong connection, sew the floss three times through the toggle bead and fabric loop. Optionally, leave an embroidery floss tail, knotted or not, for added detail.

8. Trim any excess thread along the seams with the scissors. For added style, twist the fabric strips together loosely before wearing.

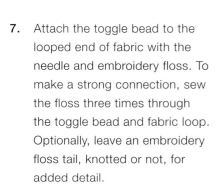

DESIGNER
Gögçe Kayihan

Fleur de Leaf Brooch

These silk "leaves" show how an organic inspiration can lead to an elegantly tailored result. Look for fabrics with colors like the ones here to evoke the splendor of autumn, or go for bolder shades to capture the promise of spring.

Try This

1. If you chose lightweight fabric, boil the starch solution until it's clear, and then pour it into a plastic bowl. Add the fabric and let it soak. Remove the fabric and iron it at the correct setting until it's dry and smooth. If you chose heavyweight fabric, it doesn't need to be starched; simply iron the fabric at the appropriate heat until it's smooth and wrinkle-free.

2. On a hard surface, use the ruler to mark five 3-inch (7.6 cm) squares of fabric. Cut them out.

3. Fold one square piece diagonally. Fold it again diagonally to form a smaller triangle. Close the necklace by carefully placing both ends of the cord between the last matching pair of circles. Fuse them together.

Get This

Silk, cotton, or rayon kimono fabric (see Tip), 6 x 9 inches (15.2 x 22.9 cm)

Circle of stiffened felt, 1½ inches (3.8 cm) in diameter

Metal pin back

Starch solution (1 tablespoon starch in 1 quart [.95 liters] of water)

Ruler

Scissors

Rotary blade and cutting mat (optional)

Tweezers

Hot glue and glue gun

Plastic bowl

TIP: Choose lightweight fabrics for a crisp look. For a softer look, choose heavier fabrics, similar to upholstery fabric.

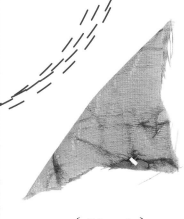

{ Fig. 1 }

{ Fig. 2 }

{ Fig. 3 }

{ Fig. 4 }

4. Hold the folded triangle with the tweezers and cut off the bottom edge to make the fabric even (figure 1). Apply hot glue along the edge of the fabric so that all of the folds stick together. Let the glue cool and dry completely before continuing.

5. Repeat steps 3 and 4 for the other fabric squares.

6. Fold one triangle of fabric horizontally and press it to form a crease (figure 2). Unfold it. Following the crease, fold the tip of the triangle outward and press it with your fingers (figure 3). Hold the base of the crease for support. Repeat for all five triangles to create five "leaf" shapes.

7. Place one "leaf" (leaf #1) on its left side. Apply hot glue, starting from the bottom, on 30 percent of the right edge of the leaf, and quickly place another leaf (leaf #2) on top so that the right edge of the first leaf and left edge of the second are parallel. Hold them together until the glue is dry, making sure the other leaf edges are free of glue (figure 4).

8. Flip the two leaves over and apply a line of hot glue on 30 percent of the left edge of leaf #1, again from the bottom. Quickly align the right edge of leaf #3 with the left edge of leaf #1. Hold the edges together and give the glue time to set.

9. Flip the leaves over again, put hot glue on 30 percent of the right edge of leaf #2. Quickly add leaf #4, aligning the right edge of leaf #2 and left edge of leaf #4. Hold them together until the glue is dry.

10. Flip the leaves over and apply a line of hot glue on 30 percent of the left edge of leaf #3. Add the final leaf, #5 parallel to leaf #3. Hold them together and let the glue set. The whole piece should now look like a five-leaf arrangement (figure 5).

11. Apply hot glue to the back of the leaves to attach the circle of stiffened felt. When the glue is dry, place a 1-inch (2.5 cm) line of hot glue in the middle of the felt and quickly press the pin back on it (figure 6).

Lily Yung
Fiddle Head, **2007**

183 x 5 x 0.2 cm
Wool felt; laser cut
Photos by artist

Origami Earrings

These earrings were inspired by origami, the Japanese art of paper folding. In Japan, most people learn the technique, often at a young age. This project applies the craft to kimono fabric.

Get This

- 2 pieces of different-color kimono print fabric, 6 inches (15.2 cm) square or larger
- Scrap paper, about 3 inches (7.6 cm) square
- 146 gold-colored seed beads
- 8 black seed beads
- 6 black crystal beads, 4 mm
- 4 gold-on-red round beads, 5 mm
- 2 gold-plated sterling silver earring hooks
- Polyester sewing thread
- 24-gauge gold-colored round wire, at least 3 inches (7.6 cm) in length
- Fabric-marking pen
- Thin bead needle
- Sewing machine
- Hand-sewing needle
- Jewelry pliers with wire cutter
- Fabric scissors
- Rotary cutter and mat (optional)

Try This

Making the Fabric Flower

1. Fold the scrap of paper into an equilateral triangle with 2¾-inch (7 cm) sides, which includes a ¼-inch (6 mm) seam allowance. Place the two pieces of fabric with right sides together, on a flat surface or cutting mat. Put the triangular paper pattern on the fabrics and trace around it with a fabric-marking pen; cut the fabrics on the marking.

2. Machine- or hand-sew the two fabric pieces together with a ¼-inch (6 mm) seam allowance, leaving ¾-inch (1.9 cm) unstitched in the center of one side.

97

{ Fig. 1 }

{ Fig. 2 }

{ Fig. 3 }

{ Fig. 4 }

3. Turn the triangle right side out, making sure the three corners are fully extended and flat. Hand sew the opening closed (figure 1).

4. Fold the three corners into the center and hand sew them together (figure 2) with tiny straight stitches.

5. Turn the piece over. Gather the centers of the three flat areas from the other side and sew them together in the center to form a flower (figure 3).

6. Sew one gold-on-red bead onto the center of the flower. Turn it over and sew another one onto the center of the other side (figure 4).

Beading Above the Flower

7. Cut a 1¼-inch (3.2 cm) length of the gold-colored wire. Bend one end into a closed loop, using the jewelry pliers. String beads on the wire in the following order: 5 gold-colored seed beads, 1 black seed bead, and 5 more gold-colored seed beads. Close the open end of the wire by bending it into a loop. Cut off any excess wire.

8. Attach the gold-plated sterling silver earring hook to one end of the wire. Sew the remaining end to the top (one of the triangle points) of the fabric flower.

Beading Below the Flower

9. Thread the thin bead needle with at least 12 inches (30.5 cm) of the sewing thread. Make a knot and push the needle through the top of either gold-on-red bead. String 10 gold-colored seed beads onto the thread and push them close to the gold-on-red bead.

10. Next, string the following beads onto the thread: 1 black 4-mm bead, 12 gold-colored seed beads, 1 black seed bead, 14 gold-colored seed beads, 1 black 4-mm bead, and finally 1 gold-colored seed bead.

11. Holding the last gold-colored seed bead in place, insert the needle back through the bottom black crystal bead and run it all the way back through all the beads, including the gold-on-red bead. After sewing a few stitches out of sight to attach the string to the flower, knot and cut the thread.

12. Turn the flower over and repeat step 9, threading the needle through the same 10 gold-colored beads and add one black 4-mm bead.

13. Now add the following new beads: 8 gold-colored seed beads, 1 black seed bead, 8 gold-colored seed beads, 1 black seed bead, 9 gold-colored seed beads, 1 black 4-mm bead, and 1 gold-colored seed bead. Then repeat step 11.

14. Repeat all of the steps to make the second earring.

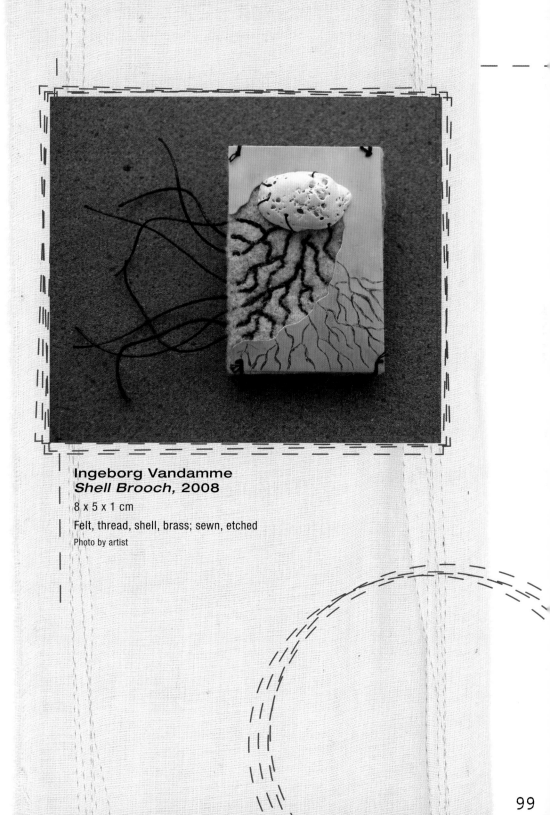

Ingeborg Vandamme
Shell Brooch, 2008
8 x 5 x 1 cm
Felt, thread, shell, brass; sewn, etched
Photo by artist

Collar to Cuff

If you have an old sweater with an attractive collar, you can recycle the collar to make this exquisite bracelet. Because sweaters come in so many different fabrics, colors, and textures, you can make an unlimited variety of bracelets using this same technique. What's in *your* closet?

Try This

1. Carefully cut the collar from the sweater, leaving approximately ⅜ inch (1 cm) of the sweater material attached. Cut the collar to a length of 8½ inches (21.6 cm). The width of the bracelet depends on the size of the collar.

2. Cut two pieces of the black glitter felt (figure 1): 2 x 9½ inches (5.1 x 24.1 cm) and 2 x 4 inches (5.1 x 10.2 cm).

{ Fig. 1 }

Get This

Sweater collar with a finished edge, 2 to 2¾ inches (5.1 to 7 cm) wide

9 x 12-inch (22.9 x 30.5 cm) sheet of black glitter craft felt

⅜-inch (1 cm) shank button

Hank of silver-lined bugle beads, size 3/0

Black sewing thread

Scissors

Ruler

Dressmaker pins

Sewing machine (Optional)

Sewing needle and thread

Seam ripper

#12 beading needle, 1½ to 2 inches (3.8 to 5.1 cm) long

TIP: If you don't have something in your closet you can use, remember most thrift stores and garage sales have a wonderful selection of old sweaters you can scavenge.

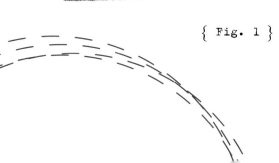

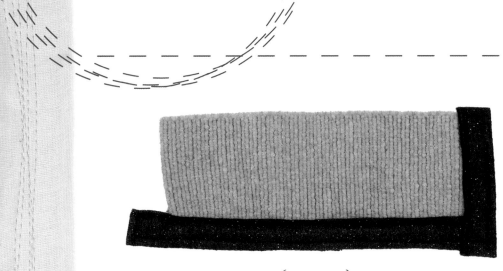

{ Fig. 2 }

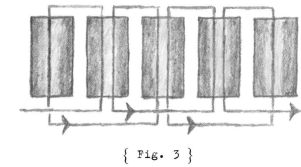

{ Fig. 3 }

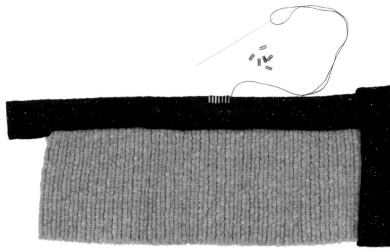

{ Fig. 4 }

3. Sew both pieces of felt to the raw edges of the collar, leaving a 1-inch (2.5 cm) felt tail past the collar on one end. Topstitch the outer edge of the felt with a ⅛-inch (3 mm) seam allowance for this and all sewing. When finished, both sides of the collar should look the same (figure 2).

TIP: If the two sides don't match and the felt on the back is uneven, trim the extra material to correspond with the line of sewing.

4. Thread the #12 beading needle with 1 yard (91.4 cm) of sewing thread. Start anywhere along the edge of the black felt and stitch the bugle beads side by side to cover both the inner and outer edge of the felt using the bugle fence stitch (figure 3). To do this, stitch through the fabric and then through the beads a couple of times to stabilize the beads and secure them to the felt and each another (figure 4).

5. Attach the ⅜-inch (1 cm) shank button. Any shank button that compliments your design will work. Stitch the button to the bracelet at the point where the two black pieces of felt overlap.

6. To make the buttonhole, measure about ¼ inch (6 mm) from the end of the felt tail and use the seam ripper to cut a slit through both pieces of material. Cut slowly and make sure the button fits through the slit easily, but take care not to cut the slit too long. Buttonhole stitch around the slit to finish the edges. Sew around twice for better support, if desired. Optionally, you can make a buttonhole by machine.

DESIGNER
Mieko Mintz

Pleated Posy Necklace

Surrounded by mountains of leftover fabric? Use a spare pleated piece or two to make this eye-catching necklace. So dig into your mountain and scour your scrap drawer. Waste not, want not.

Try This

Making the Pleated Fabric Flowers

1. Cut two pieces of fabric 1¾ x 4 inches (4.4 x 10.2 cm) for the large flowers. Make sure the cut length is perpendicular to the pleats. Cut two pieces 1½ x 3½ inches (3.8 x 8.9 cm) for the medium flowers. Cut three pieces ¼ x 3 inches (6 mm x 7.6 cm) for the small flowers.

Get This

- Pleated fabric, at least 12 inches (30.5 cm) square
- ⅜-inch (1 cm) suede tape, at least 42 inches (106.7 cm) long
- Polyester sewing thread in a matching color
- 26-gauge round wire, at least 15 inches (38.1 cm) long
- Batting or other soft material (for filling the "flower buds")
- Sewing machine
- Hand-sewing needle
- Jewelry pliers with wire cutter
- Fabric scissors

{ Fig. 1 }

{ Fig. 2 }

{ Fig. 3 }

2. For each flower piece, machine-stitch the short ends, with right sides together to make a loop (figure 1). Fold the outside edge from front to back, creating a ¼-inch (6 mm) seam and sew it down all the way around.

3. In the center of one large and one medium flower, also fold a ¼-inch (6 mm) seam from the front side to the back of the fabric. Sew it down, leaving a ½-inch (1.3 cm) opening for the wire (figure 2).

4. For the other five flowers, fold a ¼-inch (6 mm) seam in the opposite direction (back to front). Again, leave a ½-inch (1.3 cm) opening for the wire.

5. Cut seven 3-inch (7.6 cm) pieces of round wire, one for each flower. With the jewelry pliers, curl each wire into a circle. Push each wire through the opening in a flower's outer seam. Twist the wire ends together and cut off any excess so the wire doesn't show. Sew the opening closed (figure 3).

Making the Flower Buds

6. Cut four pieces of fabric, 1¾ x 2 inches (4.4 x 5.1 cm) for the flower buds. Make sure the length is perpendicular to the pleats. Machine-stitch the ends of each piece with right sides together (lengthwise) to make a loop.

7. On each loop, fold ¼-inch (6 mm) on the outside edge of the circle from the front side to the back of the fabric. Hand-sew a running stitching along the fold. Keep the needle threaded. Pull the thread and gather the fabric tightly together to create a ball shape. Knot the end of the thread and cut off the excess.

{ Fig. 4 }

{ Fig. 5 }

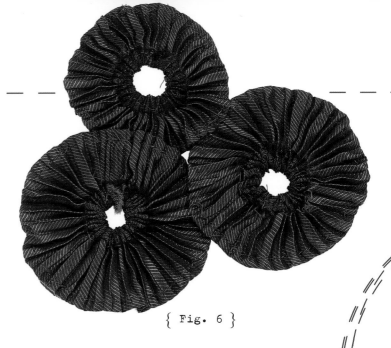

{ Fig. 6 }

8. Turn the fabric of one piece inside out to show the front of the fabric. On the open side, sew another ¼-inch (6 mm) seam, again front to back, keeping the needle threaded. Stuff enough batting inside the fabric to make a ball. Cut a 3-inch (7.6 cm) length of suede and push one end inside the ball. Pull the thread and gather this end tightly together. Sew this side shut, sewing through the suede tape. Make a knot in the tape and push it down against the top of the ball (figure 4). Repeat this step to finish the three other buds.

Making the Leaves

9. Cut four pieces of fabric 1½ x 2 inches (3.8 x 5.1 cm). Make sure the length is perpendicular to the pleats. Along the two long sides of each piece, fold a ¼-inch (6 mm) seam from the front to the back, and then sew it closed.

10. Cut four 7-inch (17.8 cm) pieces of the round wire. Push one through a seam of one fabric flower. Then bend the wire with the jewelry pliers to match the curve of the leaf tip. Pull out the wire and push it back in on both sides. Curl the wire on the side of the leaf to match that curve. Twist the ends together and cut off the excess wire. Sew both ends shut to make the tips of the leaf (figure 5).

Putting It All Together

11. Using small stitches, sew one medium and two large flowers together, overlapping along the edges (figure 6). Sew on two leaves at the bottom, and then sew a leaf and two flowers on each side, above the three central flowers (refer to the project photo).

12. Hand-sew two flower buds to the bottom of the central flowers by attaching the tape to the back of a flower. Then sew one bud to the back of a leaf on each side of the necklace. Cut two more pieces of the suede tape, each 15 inches (38.1 cm) long. Sew one end of each tape to the back of the top flower on each side (see the project photo again). To wear the necklace, tie the free ends to the desired length.

Carefree Bead Bangle

Sweet and playful, this project—with its fabric-covered wooden beads—evokes the nostalgic look of the curtains in a country kitchen, or the pattern of a well-worn sundress. Make a single bracelet in your favorite fabric, or mix and match two or three in a classic combination.

Get This

Lightweight gingham fabric, 2 x 19½ inches (5.1 x 49.5 cm)

Sewing thread in a coordinating or contrasting color

About 12 wooden beads, ½ inch (1.3 cm) in diameter

13 clear orthodontic rubber bands, ⅛ inch

Fray retardant

Sewing machine

Scissors

Straight pins

Large safety pin

Finding Supplies

Wooden beads are easy to find in the woodworking section of most craft and hobby supply shops. The number of beads determines the diameter of the finished project; 12 beads create a bracelet that's about 7¾ inches (19.7 cm) long or 3 inches (7.6 cm) in diameter. Make sure you buy clear orthodontic rubber bands. Typically they are an amber-yellow color that might detract from your finished project. For help finding them, check our list of sources at www.larkbooks.com.

Try This

1. Thread the sewing machine and set it for small, straight stitches. Choose matching or contrasting thread colors, to your taste. To add a bit of whimsy to a black-and-white bracelet, for example, try an unexpected thread color.

2. Fold the fabric strip in half with right sides together and cut edges aligned. Pin it closed with the straight pins (figure 1).

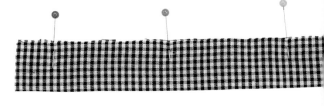

{ Fig. 1 }

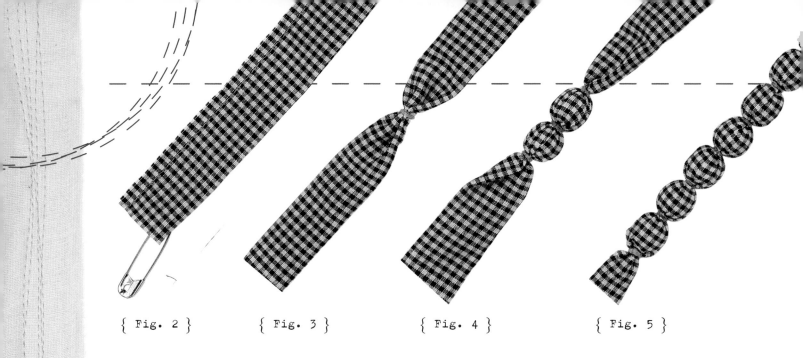

{ Fig. 2 }   { Fig. 3 }   { Fig. 4 }   { Fig. 5 }

3. Stitch a straight seam ¼ inch (6 mm) from the open side of the folded fabric. Backstitch at the beginning and end. Check the width of the fabric tube you just made by sliding a wooden bead all the way through. If the bead doesn't fit smoothly, remove the stitching and try again, with a smaller seam allowance this time.

4. Turn the fabric tube right side out. To do this easily, attach the safety pin to one end and pull it through the tube. Flatten the tube and center the seam as best you can. Do not iron; you don't want a pressed seam.

5. Sew a small seam to close the tube about 3½ inches (8.9 cm) from one end (figure 2). Wrap one orthodontic rubber band around the tube at the seam. I like to wrap the bands twice around the fabric (figure 3).

6. Drop a wooden bead into the open end of the tube and guide it down to the closed end. Holding the bead and fabric tightly in place, wrap another orthodontic band around the tube to seal the bead in the tube.

7. Repeat step 6 until you've used all the wooden beads (figures 4 and 5). The bracelet will fit most small-to-medium adult wrists. Add or subtract beads to customize the bracelet to the desired size.

8. Stitch the tube closed, as close as possible to the last bead. Backstitch at the beginning and end of the seam.

9. Tie the two ends of the tube together with a simple square knot. Cut the dangling ends, leaving a 1½-inch (3.8 cm) tail on each side (figure 6). Trim any loose threads and apply a fray retardant to seal the inside seams and to keep the fabric from unraveling.

{ Fig. 6 }

Myung Urso
Neckpiece, Poem, **2007**

30.5 x 30.5 x 5 cm

Cotton, oriental ink, sterling silver; calligraphy, hand sewn

Photo by Dan Neuberger

111

DESIGNER
Alysse Hennessey

Sun-Kissed Lemons

No matter what the time of year, this citrus-inspired necklace will lift your spirits. Have fun with the fabric collage technique and free-motion stitching you'll use to compose and personalize this artful still life.

Get This

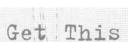

Cardboard, 3½ inches (8.9 cm) square

Cotton scraps or 6-inch (15.2 cm) strips of yardage, in four shades of yellow, white, dark green, light green, and lavender

6-inch (15.2 cm) cuts of polar fleece, in yellow and green

Double-sided heat-and-bond fusing with paper backing

2 spools of thread in variegated colors: lavender/purple and yellow/gold

Heat-and-bond light fusing

5 strands of yarn, any variety, each about 34 inches (86.4 cm) in length

Sewing machine

Sharp fabric scissors

TIP: When selecting the fabrics, choose three colors that resemble a typical lemon. Hand-dyed or variegated prints, a tiny calico, or solids all will work beautifully. Pick out a white for highlights and a dark yellow to add depth. Go bold with this color!

Try This

Creating the Lemon Shapes

1. Draw the outline of a lemon, about 2 x 3 inches (5.1 x 7.6 cm), on the piece of cardboard. Nature is irregular so perfection is unnecessary. If you wish, copy the template on page 140. Cut out the template.

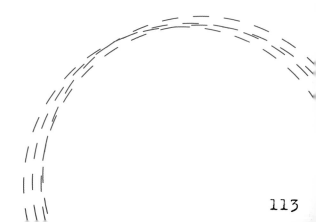

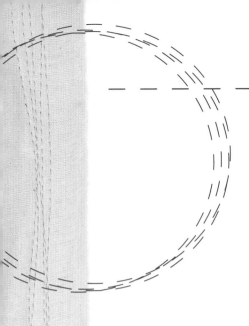

{ Fig. 1 }

{ Fig. 2 }

2. Cut a 6 x 12-inch (15.2 x 30.5 cm) piece of a yellow fabric for the base of the necklace. Loosely trace the lemon pattern five times on the fabric, at least ½ inch (1.3 cm) apart and away from any edge (figure 1). Flip the template over to trace two of the lemons, for variety. Also, draw a 2-inch (5.1 cm) diameter circle to act as a lemon slice.

3. Apply the fusible web to the back of the other three yellow fabrics and the white fabric, following the manufacturer's instructions. Let the fabric cool and then peel the paper off.

TIP: The name of the game here is to fuse the fabrics, not your iron. If you accidentally melt some fusible backing onto your iron, wipe it off on a fabric scrap while the iron is still hot. Brush off your ironing board when you are done.

4. Cut out small, irregular shapes from two of the yellow fabric pieces with the fusible web on the back (not the fabric with the lemon shapes). Make two piles. Do not cut any shape smaller than your fingertip or larger than a lemon quarter.

5. Lay the irregular shapes fusible side down on the lemon shapes in the first fabric, overlapping the template lines and each other. Don't pile them too thick, or you

won't be able to sew through them (figure 2). Create the lemon slice with cut shapes that point into the center to form rough lemon sections.

6. Lightly fuse the fabric shapes down with a hot dry iron, pressing for three seconds only. Press and lift; don't slide the iron or the shapes will slide too.

7. Cut long irregular pieces from the darkest yellow fabric that has fusible web on the back. Then place them on the lower half of each lemon. Cut three or four small shapes from the white fabric and place them along the top half of each lemon. Also cut three small, white seed shapes and place them on the cut lemon. Fuse these fabric shapes down over the previous shapes, holding the iron for a count of six.

Stitching the Lemons

8. Lay the lemon fabric on the yellow fleece backing and pin them together between the lemon shapes. Trim away any extra fleece.

9. Install a sharp new needle and adjust your sewing machine. Drop the feed dogs and change to the correct presser foot that enables you to stitch freely over the fabric in all directions by moving it with your hands. If the thread breaks, loosen the tension or use a better quality thread. Follow your machine's manual for more information on free-motion stitching.

10. Lightly doodle-stitch all over the lemons, even going outside the lines. There are no lines or patterns that must be followed; there is no right or wrong. When doodling over the shaded half of the lemons, use a darker, orange-yellow thread. Use the white thread over the white shapes. When stitching over the lemon slice, doodle in the sections, like slices of a pizza. Relax and sew smoothly at a medium speed.

11. Cut out the lemons, just inside the template lines so they don't show. Finish the edges of each lemon by sewing a wide zigzag stitch with the variegated thread. Line up the fabric so the machine's needle falls off the fabric to the right on each stitch, which then wraps the edges, creating a fun, textural finish.

Making the Leaves

12. Draw a 1½ x 2½-inch (3.8 x 6.4 cm) leaf pattern on the cardboard, or trace the template on page 140. Sketch in fat, spiky veins. Cut it out.

13. Cut a 3 x 10-inch (7.6 x 25.4 cm) strip from each of the light green, dark green, and lavender fabrics. Add fusing to the back of these strips, and then trace five leaves on each fabric, using the template. To create the thick veins for each leaf in lavender, use a disappearing ink pen to mark the veins or just cut out the whole leaf shape, then trim it down to get the veins (figure 3). Cut out five small half-leaves from the light green and dark green fabrics.

14. Cut out a 6 x 12-inch (15.2 x 30.5 cm) rectangle from the green fleece. Loosely trace the leaf template on it five times. Layer the leaf fabrics—light green and dark green with the lavender vein system on top—on the green fleece, within the leaf outline. Vary the side of the leaf on which you place the light green half (figure 4). Pin the fabric, and then fuse the layers together.

{ Fig. 3 }

{ Fig. 4 }

15. Set your machine to free-motion (see step 9), and stitch the leaves with variegated purple thread. Trace over and elongate the veins, adding even more veins with the thread.

16. Cut out the leaves, and finish the edges with a wide zigzag, positioning the needle to fall off the fabric and wrap the leaf (see step 11). To add highlights, use light green thread to zigzag the light green side of the leaves. To add shadows, use dark green thread on the dark green side.

Assembling the Necklace

17. Cut five strands of scrap yarn, each 34 inches (86.4 cm) long. Cut a 16 x 3-inch (40.6 x 7.6 cm) rectangle of the dark green fabric and wrap it, right sides together, around one end of the yarn hank. Sew down the length of the fabric and then turn the corner to sew over the yarn at the end of the fabric, leaving half the yarn sticking out the bottom. Don't sew too closely to the yarn, or you won't be able to turn it right side out. Trim the seam allowance to ⅙ inch (4 mm) and slide the fabric down over the yarn to be right side out. Cut off the excess yarn. Place one leaf at the end of the cord, overlapping it by ½ inch (1.3 cm) with the cord in the back. Sew them together from the top.

18. Lay out the lemons, overlapping one another in a pleasing arc, with the lemon wedge in front. Add all the leaves except one and pin the pieces together. You might find it easier to pin the pieces into two smaller groups and then sew the two groups together. Consider leaving some leaf edges unattached. Use clear thread and a straight stitch to attach the pieces, sewing just inside the zigzag where the pieces overlap.

Connecting the Clasp

19. In the top right lemon, sew a buttonhole large enough to pull a folded leaf through. To hand sew a buttonhole, cut the hole and whipstitch over the raw edges by hand (page 24). Size the necklace and cut the cord to size. Sew one end firmly behind the top left lemon and the other end to the last leaf, at the stem end. Put on the necklace and pull the loose leaf through the buttonhole to hold the necklace closed.

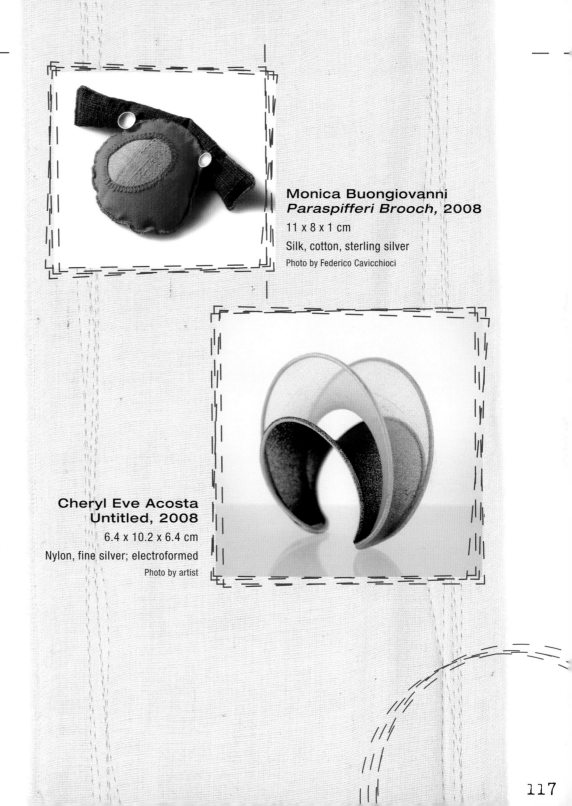

Monica Buongiovanni
Paraspifferi Brooch, 2008
11 x 8 x 1 cm
Silk, cotton, sterling silver
Photo by Federico Cavicchioci

Cheryl Eve Acosta
Untitled, 2008
6.4 x 10.2 x 6.4 cm
Nylon, fine silver; electroformed
Photo by artist

Big Rock Brooches

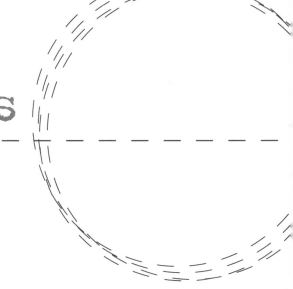

Even the Hope Diamond is no longer beyond your reach. When you make this nifty brooch, you get to size the gems as large as you want. Here's some bling you can feel good about—it's all the sparkle and none of the shame.

Get This

- 2 photos of a gem or jewel (one larger than the other)
- Iron-on photo transfer sheets (compatible with your printer)
- Cream-colored satin, ¼ yard (22.9 cm) or large scrap
- Gold-colored satin, ¼ yard (22.9 cm) or large scrap
- Felt (matching "gem" color), 9 x 12 inches (22.9 x 30.5 cm)
- Double-sided iron-on adhesive sheets
- Invisible and gold-colored thread
- Polyester fiberfill
- Firm stabilizer fabric, ¼ yard (22.9 cm)
- 1-inch (2.5 cm) pin back
- 12-mm jump ring
- Gold-leafing paint pen
- Scissors
- Iron and ironing board
- Sewing machine
- Basting glue stick
- Hot glue and glue gun
- Small hole-punch
- 2 flat-nose pliers

Try This

Making the Large Gem

1. Save the photo of the gem to your computer. Use a photo program to size the gem to the desired size. Print the image onto the transfer sheet.

TIP: You can also take your chosen image and a transfer sheet to your local print shop. They will help you make a perfect copy in just the right size.

{ Fig. 1 }

{ Fig. 2 }

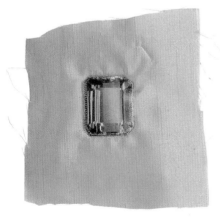

{ Fig. 3 }

2. Cut out the image of the gem, leaving a 1- to 1½-inch (2.5 to 3.8 cm) paper border all around. Follow the manufacturer's instructions to transfer the image onto the cream satin (figure 1).

TIP: Light-colored fabric keeps the gem colors looking bright. Shiny satin makes the gem sparkle. Familiarize yourself with the transfer paper by making a few practice samples.

3. Cut a piece of the iron-on adhesive slightly smaller than the gem. Iron it onto the back of the satin. Carefully cut out the gem, right along the edge.

4. Remove the paper backing from the adhesive. Place the gem face down on the ironing board with a piece of the gold satin right side down on top of it. Iron them together. Trim away the extra gold fabric, leaving a 1- to 1½-inch (2.5 to 3.8 cm) fabric border around the gem (figure 2).

5. With the invisible thread in the top of the sewing machine and the gold-colored thread in the bobbin, stitch a very small zigzag stitch all the way around the edge of the gem, catching both the gem and the gold fabric (figure 3).

6. Lay the gem on top of the stabilizer fabric and cut the stabilizer fabric to the size of the gold satin. Machine-stitch the gold fabric to the stabilizer, right next to the gem. Leave 1 inch (2.5 cm) unstitched (figure 4). Stuff a small amount of the fiberfill into the opening—just enough to gently puff out the gem—and machine-stitch the opening closed.

7. From underneath, cut away the excess stabilizer as close as possible to the stitching. Cut evenly; any lumps or bumps will show up later. Now, cut the gold satin all the way around the gem, leaving a ½-inch (1.3 cm) border.

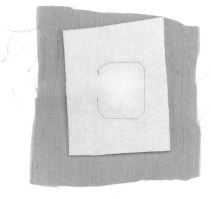

{ Fig. 4 }

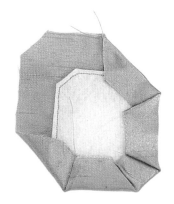

{ Fig. 5 }

{ Fig. 6 }

Making the Small Gem

8. Fold the gold satin to the back, over the stabilizer and secure it with the basting glue. Basting glue holds fabric without gumming up the machine's needle and it's repositionable. Smooth the fabric so it lays flat without folds along the edge, especially on the round edges. Lift and stretch the fabric as needed (figure 5).

9. Lay the piece right side up on the felt. Machine-stitch around the gem once again to attach it to the felt. Trim the felt off as close as possible to the stitching.

10. Hot glue the pin back to the felt. Cut a small piece of felt that fits through the pin back and extends ½ inch (1.3 cm) on either side. Hot glue it in place.

11. Save the photo of the gem to your computer. Use a photo program to size the gem to the desired size. Print the image onto the transfer sheet.

12. Cut out the image of the gem leaving a 1- to 1½-inch (2.5 to 3.8 cm) paper border all around and follow the manufacturer's instructions to transfer the image onto the cream satin. Using the gold-leafing pen, carefully fill in ¾ inch (1.9 cm) around the gem.

13. Cut a piece of the stabilizer that is larger then the gold-painted area. Place the gem on top of the stabilizer, right side up. With the invisible thread in the top of the sewing machine and the gold-colored thread in the bobbin, machine-stitch on the painted gold as close as you can to the gem. Leave 1 inch (2.5 cm) unstitched (figure 6).

14. Lightly stuff a small amount of the fiberfill into the opening and machine-stitch it closed. From underneath the gem, cut off the stabilizer as close as possible to the stitching. Cut evenly; any lumps or bumps will show up later. Now, leaving a ½-inch (1.3 cm) border of gold paint, cut the satin all the way around the gem.

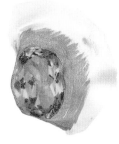

{ Fig. 7 }

15. Fold the painted fabric to the back of the gem and hold in place with hot glue. You must ease the fabric around the edge to avoid folds (figure 7).

16. Cut a piece of the felt a bit larger than the gem. Apply hot glue on the back of the gem, especially around the edge. Place the gem on the felt and press it down to set the glue. Trim the felt as close to the edge of the gem as possible.

17. Punch a small hole as close to the bottom edge (but not on the stitching) of the large gem as possible, using the hole-punch. Repeat at the top edge of the small gem.

TIP: You can print the same gem twice and iron the second gem on a different piece of satin, instead of felt, for a two-sided gem. Hot glue it in position, the same way you did with the felt.

Connecting the Gems

18. Open the jump ring and run it through the two holes to join the large gem to the small gem. Close the jump ring.

Natalia Gomensoro
Fuego Bracelet, 2006

24.1 x 12.7 x 0.3 cm

Silk, magnet closure; hand embroidered,
chain stitched

Photo by Anron Phillips

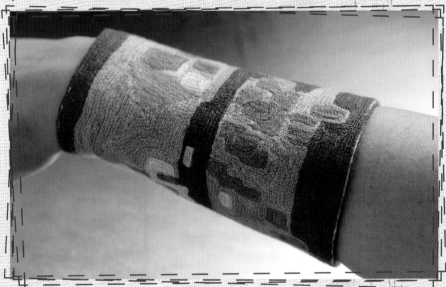

Natalia Gomensoro
Lights Bracelet, 2006

24.1 x 12.7 x 0.3 cm

Silk, magnet closure; hand embroidered, chain stitched

Photo by Anron Phillips

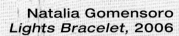

Sterling Stitches

These earrings are big and bold. Composed of mostly fabric and leather, they are also extremely lightweight. Best of all, they are eco-friendly, since you can make them out of recycled scraps.

Get This

- Lightweight fabric scrap
- Leather pieces
- Copy paper
- Ballpoint pen
- Ruler
- Paper scissors
- Small, inexpensive paintbrush
- White craft glue
- 20-gauge sterling silver, dead soft, 16 inches (40.6 cm) in length

- 24-gauge fine silver, 28 inches (71.1 cm) in length
- Sharp fabric scissors
- Hammer and a small nail
- Wood block
- Sewing machine needle, size 14
- 2 chain-nose pliers
- Round-nose pliers
- Wire cutters
- Ball peen hammer
- Steel bench block

TIP: For these earrings, you can experiment with silk, cotton, and rayon: all lightweight fabrics. If you shorten a dress or skirt, you can make matching earrings from the extra material. The leather (or vinyl) adds strength and finish to the earrings, but don't use leather that's more than a millimeter thick. You can forage for both fabric and leather scraps at your favorite thrift store or craft shop.

Try This

Making and Using the Template

1. Following the project photo, draw
    a template for the earring shape.
    Using the ruler, draw a vertical line
    that splits the shape in half. Fold
    the paper along that line. Cut out
    the shape, but don't throw away
    the paper "frame."

— — — — — — — —

TIP: After you get comfortable
with this technique, try creating
shapes and patterns of your own.
You can dramatically change the look
by changing the shapes.

— — — — — — — —

2. Place the fabric on a flat sur-
    face and smooth it out. Move
    the template "frame" around the
    scraps of fabric to find a pleas-
    ing design. While you need two
    pieces from the same fabric
    scrap, the designs within the fab-
    ric do not have to match. Place
    the template within the frame and
    remove the frame. Trace around
    the template with the ballpoint
    pen, holding the template firmly
    in place. Repeat for the second
    earring.

Creating the Fabric Earring

3. Using the fabric scissors, cut out
    the fabric for each earring 1/8 inch
    (3 mm) beyond the pen outline.

4. With the paintbrush, spread a
    thin coat of the white glue across
    a piece of paper large enough for
    both fabric pieces. Gently place
    both earring fabrics, one at a
    time, on the paper, over the glue,
    pressing them in place with your
    fingers. Start from the center and
    work your way out to eliminate
    bubbles. Dab or pat the fabric;
    pushing can stretch it. If the glue
    comes through to the right side,
    it will dry clear. Let the fabric
    pieces dry.

5. Cut out the pieces using the pen line as your guide. The paper keeps the fabric ends in place and provides a white canvas between the fabric and the dark leather.

6. Cut out a small piece of leather large enough to fit both pieces of fabric. Spread a thin coat of white glue across the rough side of the leather with the brush. One at a time, place the fabric/paper pieces on top of the leather with the fabric side up and finger press them to the leather. Make sure the fabric edges make good contact with the leather. When the glue is dry, cut out the shapes.

7. Using the hammer and nail, pound a small hole in the wood block about 1/16 inch (1.6 mm) wide and 1/8 to 1/4 inch (3 to 6 mm) deep. Place one of the earring pieces, fabric side up, on the wood block. Grip the thick end (the shank) of the sewing machine needle either between your thumb and index finger or between your thumb and middle finger with your index finger on top. Position the tip of the needle on the fabric about 1/32 inch (1 mm) down from the top of the teardrop shape. Slide the piece over so the needle is directly over the hole in the wood block. With controlled pressure, push the nee-dle all the way through the fabric, paper, and leather (figure 1).

8. Repeat step 7, punching holes about every 1/8 inch (2.5 mm) around the shape, 1/16 inch (1.6 mm) from the edge. You can approximate or you can mark the hole locations ahead of time (but don't use the ballpoint pen).

TIP: If you're using your index finger to press down on the needle and it starts to get sore, wear a thimble or place a scrap of leather between your finger and the needle. If you notice that the fabric is fraying, smear a bit of glue on the area.

Making the Wire Frames

9. Cut two 8-inch (20.3 cm) pieces of the 20-gauge wire. Bend one wire into a teardrop shape, using the round-nose pliers as needed. Once you've formed the basic shape, hold it up to your fabric earring and shape the wire so that it sits just inside the edge of the fabric (figure 2). With the chain-nose pliers, bend one end of the wire so it meets the other wire and holds the teardrop shape in place.

{ Fig. 1 }

{ Fig. 2 }

{ Fig. 3 }

{ Fig. 4 }

{ Fig. 5 }

10. Wrap the remaining inch (2.5 cm) of the wire twice around the other wire end to complete a coil. Cut the excess wire off at the back and hide the end. Use the round-nose pliers to bend the remaining wire—about $\frac{1}{16}$ inch (1.6 mm) above the coil—a 90° angle to the right. Create a loop in the wire at the bend. Be sure the wire lies behind the coil (figure 3).

11. With the chain-nose pliers, pull the new loop around the wire twice so that the spare wire coils around the base of the loop. Cut the wire where it meets the end of the wire from your first coil. Press it in neatly (figure 3 again).

12. Repeat steps 9 through 11 to make the second frame. Hammer the wire frames on the bench block with the flat side of the ball peen hammer to make them strong and sturdy. Do not hammer the wrapped coil. Tap a few times on an area and then continue around the piece. Do not thin the metal or stretch the shape.

Stitching the Fabric to the Wire Frames

— — — — — — —

TIP: You can use sterling silver wire for this section, but you'll need to anneal it first to make it easier to work with.

— — — — — — —

13. Cut a 14-inch (35.6 cm) length of the 24-gauge, fine silver wire. Holding a metal frame in front of a fabric piece, insert one end of the wire through the top hole of the fabric. Slide it all the way through until only 1 inch (2.5 cm) sticks out in front. Keeping hold of the fabric, the frame, and the wire tail, stitch the long end of the wire around the frame through the next hole to the right. Pull it through. Continue to stitch around the earring. At the halfway point, it may look like there's too much space between the fabric and the frame, but it will all pull together (figure 4)

{ Fig. 6 }

TIP: Keep your stitches tight and even, but don't pull so tight that you rip through the fabric. If your stitches are uneven, gently squeeze them closer or spread them apart with the chain-nose pliers. As you stitch, the fabric will develop a nice curve.

14. When you've stitched through the last open hole, push the wire through the front of the top hole, the hole with the other end of the wire sticking out. (Use the needle to widen the hole, if necessary.) Bend the end of the wire you just pushed through to rest against the back of the bead wrap (figure 5).

15. Pull the wire sticking out of the front to the right and around the back of the frame, about 1/16 inch (2 mm) below the bead wrap. Wrap it three times around and up. Cut the end at the back and push it in tight to secure the other wire. Snip off the end of the other wire that's sticking out of the wrap.

16. Repeat steps 13 through 15 to make the second earring. Attach the ear wires through the bead wrap loops of each earring to finish (figure 6).

Chia Pei Hsiao
Propagation III, 2006
20 x 18 x 9 cm
Felt
Photo by artist

DESIGNER
Ellen Gerritse

Desert Flowers

This voluminous, but featherlight neckpiece, constructed from 74 tulle, mesh, and organza squares, recalls the colors of the desert. Bring your neckline to life!

Get This

- 11 different-color pieces of tulle, organza, and mesh, each about 7⅞ inches (20 cm) square
- Matching thread for every color of fabric
- Acrylic fortifier (available in DIY stores)
- All purpose glue or fabric glue
- Spray varnish
- Wax baking paper
- Large brass clasp
- Sewing machine
- Pins
- Sewing needle
- Scissors
- Wide brush

TIP: Choose fabrics with similar tones and colors, mixing in one or two totally different colors to make the finished piece more interesting (figure 1). (The project shown uses brown and green as the "other" colors.)

{ Fig. 1 }

Try This

Making the Large Gem

1. Fold each fabric square in half to intensify its color. Set your machine to a narrow zigzag stitch and machine-stitch 100 squares, each between 1⅝ inches (4 cm) and 2 inches (5 cm) in size. Use matching color thread (figure 2). Do not cut out the squares yet.

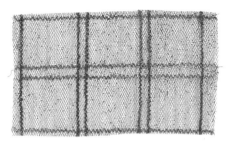

{ Fig. 2 }

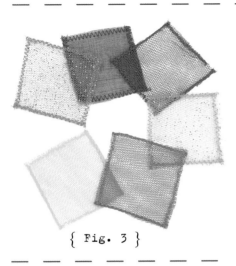

{ Fig. 3 }

{ Fig. 4 }

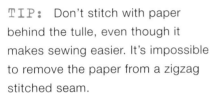

TIP: Don't stitch with paper behind the tulle, even though it makes sewing easier. It's impossible to remove the paper from a zigzag stitched seam.

2. Place a large piece of the wax paper on a flat surface. Use the brush to cover the sewn fabric pieces with the acrylic fortifier, which hardens the fabric without affecting the texture. Let them dry overnight.

3. Once the fabric is dry, cut out all the squares along the zigzag stitching lines (figure 3). For each square, bend the fabric so that two opposite corner points meet. Hand-sew together the two zigzag seams on top to create a cone shape (figure 4).

4. After you've sewn all 100 squares into cones, select 30 to glue into 15 pairs of two cones each. Randomly, but artfully match colors and sizes, and glue the cones together in different ways (for example, aligned and misaligned), but always with the open ends together.

5. Mix, match, and arrange the 15 cone pairs into two slightly bent "strings," each measuring about 7⅞ inches (20 cm). Arrange the strings so that they curve in opposite directions. Start each string with the open ends of the cones at the bottom, and then stack the following pair on top to create the curved string. Look for spots where the pairs contact each other; do not force the fabric in place.

6. When you are satisfied with the arrangement and the strings are the right length, glue the cone pairs together and let them dry. Then form a rough circle with the two strings so that the open ends of the cones point toward the center of the string. Do not glue the circle closed, as you will attach a clasp later. Glue them together and let the glue dry. This is the base of your neckpiece.

7. Now fill in the open spaces by gluing in individual cones. Always point the new cones with the open end down, facing away from the center of the circle. Glue one new cone at a time and build up the necklace. Use as many as you want until you are satisfied with the result. Make the bottom of the necklace wider (with more cones) than the sides and top. See the project photo.

8. Let the glue dry and harden completely. Then spray two or three layers of varnish over the entire piece.

9. To attach the clasp, pull the closed end of the top cone on one end of the string through the loop of the hook, fold the fabric over, and glue it in place. Pull the closed end of the other top cone on the other end of the string through the matching loop of the clasp the same way and glue the fabric down.

TIP: Use a big clasp because this neckpiece is voluminous. If you cannot find a big enough clasp, make one yourself by bending 18-gauge brass wire into an S-hook and ring.

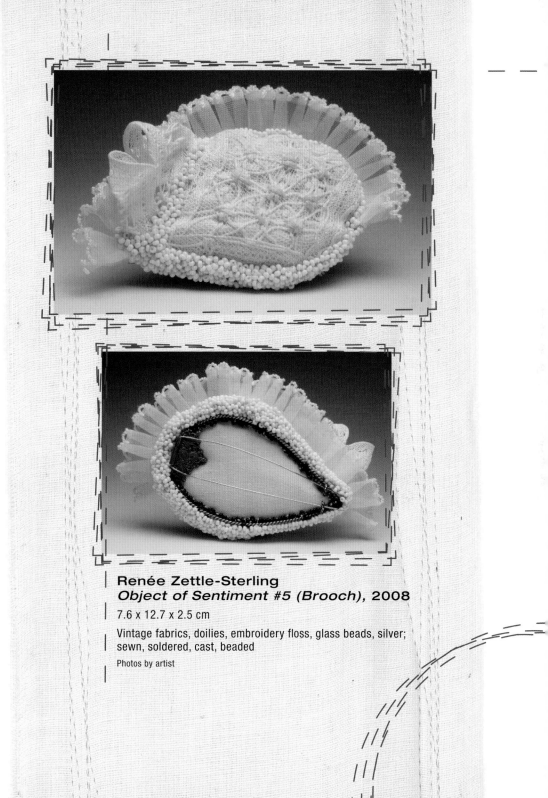

Renée Zettle-Sterling
Object of Sentiment #5 (Brooch), **2008**

7.6 x 12.7 x 2.5 cm

Vintage fabrics, doilies, embroidery floss, glass beads, silver; sewn, soldered, cast, beaded

Photos by artist

Windswept Organza Earrings

Start with silver rings, one inside another, that hold your chiffon like tiny needlepoint hoops. Dip the fabric in resin, until it hardens like a moment frozen in time. The resulting lightweight earrings are as comfortable as they are stylish.

Get This

To Make the Organza Dangles

2 pieces of silk chiffon, each 6 inches (15.2 cm) square

Clear two-part epoxy resin

Masking tape (optional)

Container for mixing resin

Fabric scissors

Single-edge razor blade

Plastic measured mixing cups

Wooden stir sticks

Safety gloves and mask

Parchment paper

Racks and wire for drying the earrings

To Make the Bezel Setting

2 sterling silver strips, 28-gauge, each ¼ x 1½ inches (6 mm x 3.8 cm)

2 sterling silver strips, 28-gauge, each ¼ x 1$\frac{19}{32}$ inches (6 mm x 4 cm)

18-gauge sterling silver round wire, six 2-inch (5.1 cm) pieces

20-gauge sterling silver round wire for earring bales

2 sterling silver French ear hooks

Scribe or fine point permanent marker

Brass bristle brush or a jewelry cleaning brush

Needle files

Flat-nose nylon jaw pliers or flat-nose pliers wrapped with masking tape

Soldering kit with medium solder

Round bezel mandrel and round ring mandrel

Bench vise

Rawhide mallet

Wet/dry abrasive paper (220, 320, 400, and 600 grit)

Wire cutters

Needle-nose pliers

Riveting hammer

Center punch

Anvil with a hole or steel block or 2 hardwood blocks

Drill press with bits with a slightly smaller diameter than the 20-gauge wire

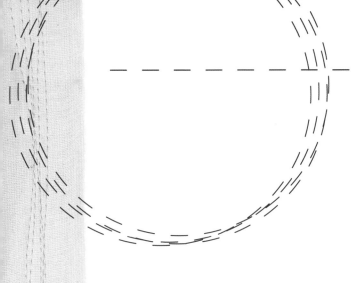

{ Fig. 1 }

{ Fig. 2 }

Try This

Making the Bezel Settings

1. Clean all of the metal strips with soap and the brass bristle brush. Gently file both ends of each strip with the needle file to make them flat.

2. Use the nylon pliers to shape each metal strip into a semi-circle, bending the two flat ends towards each other until they touch and are completely flush. You now have four unsoldered metal rings in two sizes.

3. Using the medium solder and a very gentle flame, solder the ends of each ring. After soldering, pickle the four metal rings.

4. Place the bezel mandrel in the bench vise cushioned by scrap brass. Slide one silver ring down the mandrel. Gently hammer the sides of the ring with the rawhide mallet to form a consistent shape. Be sure to hammer the bottom of the ring to avoid a conical shape. Remove the ring from the mandrel, flip it, and repeat. Switch to the ring mandrel to finish this process. Repeat this step for the other three silver rings.

5. Place the two smaller rings inside the two larger rings to make sure there is room for the fabric (figure 1). Test it with a small piece of fabric; the fabric should be taut without tearing. If necessary, change the size of the bezel. To make either ring larger, anneal the metal and then hammer the ring down the mandrel again.

6. Tape the 220-grit sandpaper to a flat surface. Sand the top and bottom of the nested rings in a circular motion, flipping the pieces over to ensure that both rings are the same height. Pull the two rings apart and gently sand the edges with a small piece of 400-grit paper. When the pieces are the same height—no shorter than ¼ inch (5.5 mm)—sand them with the 320- and 400-grit paper. Use the 600-grit paper to create a final polish on all surfaces of each ring, softening the edges so they aren't sharp, but still square (figure 2).

{ Fig. 3 }

Attaching the Fabric

7. Fold a border of tape over the edges of the silk chiffon squares to prevent the silk from fraying as you work. For a less refined look, skip this step.

8. Lay one silk square flat. Place one of the smaller, interior silver rings under the fabric in the center of the square. Loosely place the larger bezel on top of the smaller one and gently press down. You should feel some resistance, but no tearing. The overall setting should be tight, holding the fabric securely. If desired, use the rawhide mallet to very softly hammer the bezel down. The silk chiffon should drape evenly from the bezel.

9. With the razor blade, puncture the chiffon inside the bezel. Make several cuts toward the edge without scratching the silver. Lift up and cut off the little fabric triangles. Use quick shaving strokes to remove any leftover silk strands.

10. Use a torch to ball up all twelve ends of the six pieces of silver wire. Try to keep the balls very close in size. Pickle or hand-polish the balled wires. Cut the six pieces of balled wire in half with the wire cutters.

11. Place one piece of balled wire on a steel block or anvil. Gently strike the ball with the riveting hammer to create a nail head. It should only take two or three blows. Repeat to create eleven more nail heads.

12. Measure and mark eight evenly spaced points around the outside of each silver bezel. Make all marks the same height, half way between the top and bottom of the bezel. (Each bezel will have eight drilled holes, six will hold rivets and two will hold the earring bale wires.)

13. Place the bezel mandrel horizontally in the bench vise. Slide one marked bezel onto the mandrel with the fabric trailing. Using a center punch and hammer, lightly dimple each mark on the bezel to prevent the drill bit from wandering. Repeat the process on the second earring bezel.

TIP: It is important that the inside and outside rings of each bezel do not shift during step 13.

14. Choose a drill bit that is exactly the same size as the 20-gauge earring bale wire. Drill a hole straight down into one of the dimpled marks. Remove any silver filings left from the drilling. Repeat on the opposite side of the bezel. Change to a bit that is the same size as the rivet wire and drill the remaining six holes, removing the excess metal. Lightly sand the inside of the bezel with 400- and then 600-grit sandpaper. Shake the chiffon to remove any silver bits. Cover the two earring bale holes with small pieces of tape.

15. Using needle-nose pliers or tweezers, place a rivet through one of the larger drilled holes with the "nail head" on the inside. Slide the earring onto the bezel mandrel with the fabric trailing. Clip the rivet wire down to less than ³/₁₆ inch (2 mm) long. File the cut end flat, leaving about ¹/₁₆ inch (1.5 mm) of wire. Gently strike the wire with the riveting hammer to secure the rivet. Being careful with the chiffon, remove the earring from the mandrel. Repeat this step to rivet the opposite hole on the bezel. Use the same process to finish all the rivets on both earrings (see figure 3, page 137).

Applying the Resin

16. Tape parchment paper to your work surface and set up the drying racks, making sure they are tall enough to prevent the fabric from touching the surface below. Remove the tape border from the bottom of the chiffon (if used). Pull the fabric down between your index and middle finger to 2½ inches (6.4 cm). Cut just above your fingers with the fabric scissors. Snip any unattractive pieces and threads.

17. Remove the tape covering the bale holes and thread a piece of 20-gauge wire through the holes to support the earrings as they dry on the racks. Place the earrings on the racks to make sure you have space below and to become familiar with the positioning. You may choose to tape the stands to the parchment paper to increase stability.

18. Thoroughly mix the resin according to the manufacturer's directions and let it sit for 15 minutes to make it easier to apply.

TIP: Good ventilation is vital. Work under a hood or by a window with an exhaust fan. Wear a respirator with a vapor cartridge and protective gloves at all times while working with resin. You may use barrier cream to protect your hands in addition to the gloves. Have paper towels close by for wiping the resin bottles and cleaning up spills. Once you begin, you will have about an hour of working time with the resin, although you probably won't need the entire hour.

19. Hold one of the earrings in your non-dominant hand, and dip the lower part of the silk into the resin container. Using a wooden stir stick, gently push most of the fabric into the resin. Don't immerse all of the fabric. Instead, use the stir stick to paste or raise the resin onto the remaining fabric, up to but not onto the silver bezel. Pull the fabric out of the resin and remove the excess by running the stick down the fabric. Place the earring on the drying rack. Place a paper cone under the rack to support the resin-dipped fabric or use your fingers to shape the fabric in an interesting way. When the resin becomes tacky, it's time to stop working. Repeat this step for the second earring. Let the earrings dry for 24 hours in a dust-free environment. If the earring edges are sharp, apply more resin to the entire base or just the sharp parts. Then set the earring back on the racks and let it dry.

Putting It All Together

20. To make the bale, shape a 20-gauge sterling silver wire on a ⅝-inch (1.6 cm) wooden dowel into a half-round shape. Bend one end of the wire at a 90° angle with the flat-nose pliers and snip it with the wire cutters. Leave enough wire to bend and secure the bale on the inside of the bezel. Repeat on the other end. Make sure it fits. Make another one for the second earring. Place the bale ends into the two remaining holes in the earring bezel. Press the bale wire ends down onto the inside walls. Attach the store-bought French wires or your own ear-hooks.

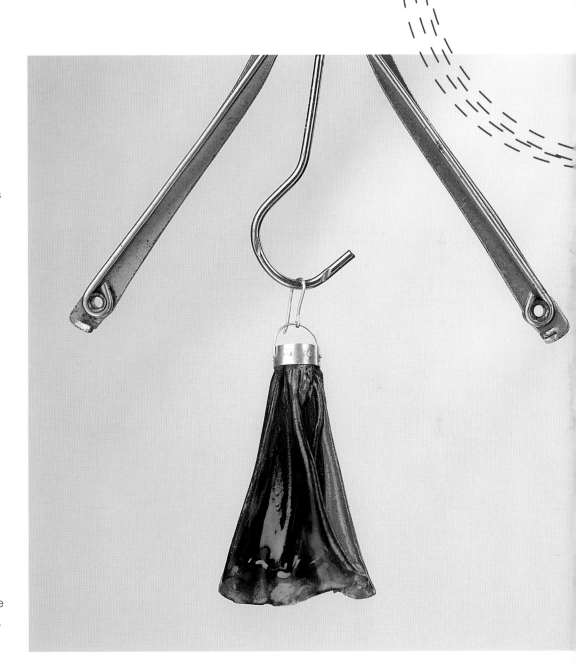

Project Templates

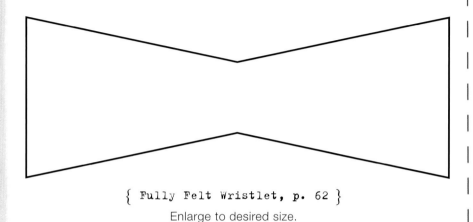

{ Fully Felt Wristlet, p. 62 }

Enlarge to desired size.

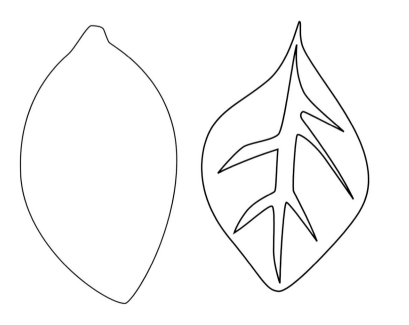

{ Sun-Kissed Lemons, p. 112 }

Enlarge to desired size.

About the Designer:

Elizabeth Beeson loves the creative process and especially likes using a variety of media and techniques. She studied art at Ball State University, Purdue University, and Herron School of Art and Design, eventually earning a master's degree in secondary education. She currently works as a high school art teacher in Indiana. You can find her work online at www.elizabethbeeson.com.

Deborah Boschert is a fiber artist who creates art quilts, fabric collages, and other bits of crafty goodness. Her work has been published in various magazines and exhibited a quilt shows and galleries around the country. She encourages others to celebrate their creative spirit through lectures, workshops, and a series of how-to books. See her work at www.deborahsstudio.com and read about her adventures at deborahsjournal.blogspot.com.

Miyuki Akai Cook gets her visual influence from wild plants. She loves transforming familiar materials into meaningful objects through knitting, crochet, and weaving—techniques she sees as metaphors of life: A handmade piece reflects the time it was made, a lasting tribute to a moment. Her work has been shown in Japan and in the US from Arizona to Massachusetts. She earned an MFA from the University of Massachusetts. See samples of her work at www.miyukiatwork.com.

As a wife and busy mother of three, **Bethany Fields** looks to everyday things for inspiration. She's been creating whimsical jewelry and artwork for as long as she can remember. Her sense of color, design, and style evolved through years of theatrical training. You can see her work at www.tvweekly.com (where she is an on-air talent and designer) and under the cute moniker Annie and Olive at www.annieandolive.etsy.com.

A silversmith/metal artist, **Sara Gallo-Cornell** is succeeding while still attending Millersville University in Lancaster County, Pennsylvania. She primarily creates one-of-a-kind art jewelry using precious metals, but she occasionally branches out to use textiles and found objects as well. To learn more about Sara's work, visit saragallo.com.

Ellen Gerritse is a world traveler who currently lives in Kuwait. Although she works primarily as a silversmith, she's taught fine arts in Europe and Asia. Ellen finds herself drawn to create objects from simple, accessible materials with a few tools she has close at hand. As a result, she loves combining her metalwork with other materials, including papier-mâché. In 2006, she won the Collectors' Choice Award during the Mind Over Metal show in Houston, Texas.

Wendi Gratz skipped home economics for wood and metal shop. She didn't learn to use a sewing machine until her college years. Her first project was a badly made tablecloth, but she learned from that disastrous experience. For her second project, she designed and made all the costumes for a play. Now she makes fun clothes, funky dolls, and all kinds of quilts. She lives in Bakersville, North Carolina, with her family and her sewing machine. You can see her work at www.wendigratz.com.

Gwen Gunther studied metalsmithing and enameling under renowned American artist Earl Pardon at Skidmore College, where she received a Bachelor of Science in Art. After a few detours, she cofounded a fashion jewelry business. Her jewelry, sold at Neiman Marcus, was published in *W* and *In Style* magazines. At the New Metals department of Corcoran College of Art & Design, she studied under Anya Pinchuk and Bob Ebendorf. Gwen is currently continuing her career as a metal artist.

On those days **Alysse Hennessey** ventures outside of her Bliss Monkey Studio, she hikes the gorgeous Pacific Northwest, designs costumes, and helps children explore textile art. She loves living in Eugene, Oregon, with her partner, two brilliant young sons, their chocolate Labrador, and two sassy hens. To catch up with her, visit alythered.etsy.com and blissmonkeystudio.blogspot.com.

Steven James, a refugee from the Midwest, showed crafting tendencies at an early age and quickly progressed beyond conventional macaroni and glitter. He now divides his time as a teacher and as a crafter, running macaroniandglitter.com. No kidding; he's got a glue gun and isn't afraid to use it. He's appeared on the HGTV and DIY networks, and his work has been featured in many publications. He loves to travel and show others how to create things to make Momma proud.

Shortly after graduating from the University of Vermont with a BA in Art and English, **Jennifer Kahn** began an apprenticeship with jewelry artist Celie Fago. Under Celie's guidance, Jennifer learned precious metal clay and metalsmithing techniques. She has since created a line of jewelry she describes as "fusing old and new, industrial and natural, urban and ethnic designs." Visit her new website at www.jenniferkahnjewelry.com.

Gögçe Ceren Kayihan, a scientist by day and artist by night, started playing with fabric when she was ten. A later embroidery class fueled her obsession. When she was introduced to the Japanese language and culture, she became enthralled. After earning her PhD, she indulged herself in "Tsumami kanzashi" and several other traditional Japanese arts. Since then, she's sold over a thousand fabric flowers while continuing to perfect her craft.

Karen J. Lauseng is an internationally recognized New Mexico artist. Her artwork has been showcased in numerous books including *The Art of Jewelry*: *Wood*, *500 Earrings*, and *The Art of Jewelry*: *Paper Jewelry* (all published by Lark Books). Her work's also appeared in many magazines, including the front cover of *Art Jewelry* magazine. She has displayed her pieces in over 100 venues including solo exhibitions, juried shows, and galleries. See for yourself at www.kjartworks.com.

Mavis Leahy has had art in her life for as long as she can remember. While she explores other creative avenues, her medium of choice is sewing with vintage textiles. She loves resurrecting these pieces of the past, many of them labors of love. Through them, she feels a strong connection with the quilters, weavers, and artisans of long ago whose beautiful textiles gain new life in her artwork. This love affair has continued through the years. Find her creations at www.turkeyred.com.

An independent artist for over a decade, **Erin Lueth** began drawing at a young age, first with charcoals and then watercolors. She went on to learn wirework, silversmithing, clothing design, felt design, knitting, and crochet. Her works have been featured in art galleries, shows, and retail stores. You can view her creations at the Sage and Daisy in Kansas City and at www.sewsewsuckurtoe.etsy.com

Born on the southern Japanese island of Kyushu, **Mieko Mintz** studied fashion in Tokyo. After 12 years working there as a fashion designer, she came to the United States to study English, and fate has kept her here ever since. She has a women's boutique in Soho in New York City. You can see her beautiful clothing and accessories at www.miekomintz.com.

Joan K. Morris once designed costumes for motion pictures, just one of the many creative paths her artistic endeavors have led her down. Her "professional hobbies" include sewing and ceramics. She has contributed projects for numerous Lark books including *Hardware Style, Hip Handbags, Beaded Home, Pretty Little Pincushions, Button Button,* and many more.

Anika Smulovitz teaches art at Boise State University, but she has exhibited across the US and in Korea. Her pieces have appeared in many magazines and books, including *The Art of Jewelry: Plastic & Resin, 500 Necklaces,* and *Fabulous Jewelry from Found Objects* (all published by Lark Books). You can view some

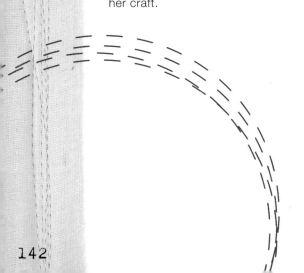

of her work at Taboo Studio in San Diego, California; Sculpture to Wear Gallery in Santa Monica, California; and J. Crist Gallery in Boise, Idaho.

Andrea Stern's family all made art in one form or another, so it was inevitable that she would make some kind of art herself. Starting with simple drawings, she eventually progressed to painting, beadwork, and quilting. While she received a formal degree in Art History in 1990, it wasn't until she owned her own bead business that she learned to apply the principles of design. Examples of her work are available at www.embellishmentcafe.com and andibeads.blogspot.com.

Designer **Sarah Terry of Guerilla Embroidery** (www.guerilla-embroidery.com) specializes in machine-embroidered textiles. Inspired by nature, each piece develops organically in fabric and thread, becoming an individual work of art. Sarah applies these ideas to bags, purses, accessories, and clothing. She graduated with a degree in Embroidery from the Manchester Metropolitan University. You can find her work in the Tate Britain and in collections all over the world.

About the Author

Marthe Le Van is a jewelry, metals, and beading editor for Lark Crafts. Since 2000, she has written, edited, juried, or curated more than 60 books. Recent publications include *21st Century Jewelry*, *Ring A Day*, and *30-Minute Rings*. Marthe has edited all jewelry books in Lark's popular "500" series and curated *500 Wedding Rings* and *Masters: Gold*. She is a member of the Art Jewelry Forum and the Society of North American Goldsmiths.

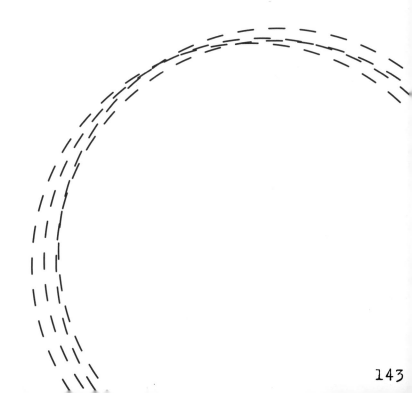

Acknowledgments

Thank you to the designers who contributed their incredible talent to this book. The exceptional quality of their projects and instructions is a true testament of their commitment to the contemporary jewelry field. I am also very grateful to the talented artists who shared images of their work to include in the book's gallery. They've provided endless inspiration to our readers and to future designers.

Many thanks to the Lark Books team that helped see *Making Fabric Jewelry* from manuscript to finished book. Larry Shea, Mark Bloom, Gavin Young, and Dawn Dillingham provided topnotch editorial support, while the art team of Stacey Budge-Kamison, Jeff Hamilton, Robin Gregory, and Chris Bryant brought the book to life through their creative vision and collaborative spirit.

Stewart O'Shields was the force behind the beautiful photography gracing these pages, and I extend special thanks for his constant ability to generate such high quality results for every publication we've worked on together.

Finally, to the art galleries, organizations, teachers, schools, and publications that so diligently advance and inspire the contemporary jewelry field at large—thank you for your unwavering enthusiasm and hard work.

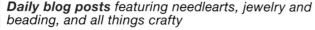

It's all on www.larkcrafts.com

Daily blog posts featuring needlearts, jewelry and beading, and all things crafty

Free, downloadable *projects* and *how-to videos*

Calls for artists and *book submissions*

A free *e-newsletter* announcing new and exciting books

...and a place to celebrate the *creative spirit*

Index